everything new

everything new

one philosopher's
search for a god
worth believing in

FOR KELLY

Because this is the second book,
And because this book is about love.

Library of Congress Cataloging-in-Publication Data

Cook, Jeff, 1976 -
Everything New : One Philosopher's Search For a God Worth Believing In / Jeff Cook.
     p. cm.

ISBN-13: 978-0615602271 (Subversive Books)
ISBN-10: 0615602274

1. Christianity 2. Eschatology 3. Philosophy   I. Title

Printed in the United States of America.
First Printing: Pentecost 2012

Subversive Books
709 16th Street
Greeley, Colorado 80631

www.subversivebooks.org

Graphic Design by Mary Emily Brink
Tricycle Concept by Betony Coons : graysparrow.com ; @betonycoons
Cover painting by Tony Garza : www.facebook.com/people/Tony-Gar-za/620246863

CONTENTS

PART ONE   AND THERE WAS EVENING

PREFACE

A lot of good people, people I think heroic and virtuous, do not believe in my God. They are my friends, my students, my colleagues. One of the latter said he thought you had to be crazy, literally nuts, to believe in a God—which doesn't make my chances at tenure look very promising.

He may be right. I teach philosophy at a state university exploring the works of writers like Russell, Hume and Nietzsche. Such thinkers continue to give me all kinds of reasons to bail God-belief (in fact by now I can argue against God's existence better than anyone else I know), but I don't find such arguments satisfying.

Strong? Sure.

Emotionally compelling? Absolutely.

I gave up God-belief during my graduate studies when I realized the religious views I had defended since high school were insufficient. But recently that changed.

When I get serious about what is real and what the best possible life looks like, I choose to believe— even after a church I worked for fell apart, even after my son was born with autism, despite the arguments and the long season in which I felt confident a God was not there. I now choose to believe not only in a God, but in a very specific God.

This is what that path has looked like.

THE NIGHT IS HERE.
THE DAY IS GONE.

The Weepies
The World Spins Madly On

1   CHAOS

On the Fourth of July, my parents' neighborhood throws a day-long celebration featuring a belly flop contest, tuba music, a massive make-your-own sloppy joe table, ice cream speed eating (cause that's good times right there), and this year someone arranged a tricycle race.

The yellow flier invited all kids six and under to take their trikes to the top of the neighborhood and race them down to the bottom of the street. The little ones would fly past teary-eyed grandparents lining the curb. The race would feature prizes, cheering, and Old Glory fluttering from behind. The vision clearly left someone in a planning committee starry-eyed.

My boys were too small to ride along, so we sat on my mom's front lawn near the finish line, waiting for some spunky kindergartner to take the checkered flag, hockey stop in the winner's circle, and pour a bottle of milk over his head—but nothing in NASCAR compares to what we saw that morning.

We heard the starter pistol and the cheers of parents in the distance. We sat looking up for a few moments, and then the wave of sixty or so children rounded the corner. From a distance you could see the determination on some of the faces as their little legs pumped the plastic pedals, their upper bodies jiggling back and forth like bobble heads. Each child was followed by a parent or two briskly walking behind, to ensure the competitors didn't bump and nothing got out of control.

The pedals of those in front were cranking, their legs looking like pistons in an old oil commercial about viscosity and thermal breakdown. As the speed of the trikes increased, parents who hadn't run since high school began to trot after their children, kindly asking them to slow down. A few stretched to catch the back of a shirt, but the gap between most racers and their guardians widened, and that's when Sir Isaac Newton decided to make things fun.

Descending toward the finish line, the street steepened and the peloton of four year olds hit what those in the elite world of tricycle racing call "The Leg/Velocity Threshold." All those tiny limbs were just going too fast, and in synchronized motion every pair of sneakers kicked away from its trike and shot out in a wide "V". The bottoms of Nikes and Keds stared at us below and sixty pairs of tricycle pedals began spinning like a fan. Faces that had been full of determination paled. Parents who had not panicked yet, panicked. A cattle stampede has more control than the sixty white knuckled preschoolers we watched tear down our hill.

And that's when they began trading paint.

Either from fear or a lack of strength, the racers began thumping into one another causing some to veer abruptly off course. One boy—with his out of shape parents huffing behind—caught an edge, took a forty-five degree angle into the curb, and flew over his handlebars into our neighbor's shrubbery. A half-dozen trikes clipped or ran straight into parked cars. A few slid sideways and capsized, but the main body of riders stayed upright, horrified and speeding toward the checkered flag.

At the finish line, wide-eyed volunteers began to squat low, preparing to catch as many of the cyclists as they could. The wave of wailing youngsters hit the tape. There was a collision, a few heavy grunts—and half the competitors kept right on rolling into the next neighborhood. Fuming parents soon followed, some showing off an impressive collection of profanities to the promoters they passed as they chased their child down the next hill.

The leftover carnage was a pure mess. From top to bottom, the street was a chaotic blend of red knees, overturned three-wheelers, and American flags. Kids were crying, parents were reaching under cars for their little one, heads were rubbed and kissed and rubbed again, and I decided that I would never buy my boys a tricycle.

SPEED

When I think about God, I don't begin with speculations about the big bang or the apparent design all around us. I don't start with miracles or my need for moral clarity. These are all secondary for me. When I first begin to think about God, I start with velocity.

I know that I am out of control. It is the most obvious detail about me.

All of us at some point ask questions about who we are and what meaning our lives have. We need something to hold on to when a friend of ours dies, or the girl we love doesn't love us back. When emotional pain hits, it is good to ask about what is real. I went through that process a while back, and I came out in a place I didn't expect. After 7 or so years of believing in a God, I began graduate studies in philosophy, eventually hitting a spot where I set God-belief aside. My agnosticism wasn't about growing up or social pressure. No one forced me to believe in a God in high school, so my new agnosticism wasn't about rebellion. I gave up God-belief because the arguments were not as compelling as I had once found them to be.

I read everything I could pointing to God's existence: through the fine-tuning of our universe, through the need for an instigator of the big bang. I wrote long papers outlining the necessity of God given the moral qualities of our world and the reality of logical laws.

These were my best efforts. It was an experiment of sorts. I stood up at one of the finest universities on earth, and held up for myself and my peers the best reasons I had to believe that God was real. I climbed that mountain, and I found there are times when you reach the top of a peak, look around and say to yourself, "Is this it? Is this really the best there is?"

The opposite side was just as compelling. Take any newspaper, any day of the week and ask the articles, "Would a good God want to stop situations like these?" The constant waves of stories and examples of human suffering made God-belief difficult.

But it was God's hiddenness that hit me most.

Looking around I saw many people I loved and respected who not only disbelieved in a God. They would often tell me that they wanted to believe but could not find a good reason to. Certainly a good God would care a great deal about my friends, I thought. But it seemed he was not doing anything to help bring such people serious insights about himself and his priorities. Perhaps the real reason God seemed distant was because he really was— and that's when I moved away from God-belief. I found what most of my atheist friends said they had already experienced. We wanted God to exist, but we just couldn't get there intellectually.

But when I surrendered God-belief, a new thing happened.

I quickly found that saying "I don't believe in God" was not like saying "I don't believe in unicorns or pixie dust." I discovered that when I said, "There is no God," I was making a claim about everything else.

When I believed in God, the world around me had purpose. It had been carefully orchestrated and it moved forward toward a goal. Stepping away from God meant an end to all that. In leaving God aside, a new vision of the world emerged. Everything, both around and within me, became mechanical, unthinking, and often chaotic.

Of course chaos can be quite beautiful, but I realized that the central truth about myself and everyone else I knew was that we were each, at the deepest levels, out of control. I saw it every day. It's not just that I could not seem to control my appetites, my mouth, my temper, my wants, my money, my health, or my ego.

Those could be chalked up as character flaws. My lack of control had a more primal cause.

The scientists tell us, and I have no trouble believing them, that human life arose from an evolutionary process in which those animals that fight, feed, and reproduce best pass on their traits. Some of those traits are slight adaptations that enhance the animal, creating really complicated things like a human personality. Some adaptations fail and the animal dies. That's the theory going, and it sounds right to me. The evidence isn't just in fossils; I can feel it in myself now. Though I might try, I cannot turn off the radar in my head searching for more sexual partners, more sugar and fats, more power, and more shelter from the unseen enemies all around me.

It has become increasingly plain to me that most of my emotions, hungers, and fears are not my own. They were handed down to me from somebody else. I didn't ask for them. They were pre-wired into my system by the evolutionary history of my ancestors. I am who I am because my forbearers destroyed their enemies, because they spread their seed, because they fed their appetites, because they were obsessive about potential dangers—and they have passed on all these obsessions to me.

Evolution, too, can be quite beautiful—in the words of one recent book it's "the greatest show on earth"—but I found my own formation deeply troubling[1]. The excessive greed and gluttony, violence and lust etched into my DNA often made me miserable. It wouldn't be so bad if fear and overconsumption, promiscuity and aggression were healthy; but I recognized that these were not signs of a good life. They were obstacles. Such tendencies made my life miserable. After giving up on a God, I found I wasn't just an animal. I recognized that I was an animal preprogrammed to think and act in self-destructive ways, ways that didn't care about "me"—only about the promotion and replication of my genes. But it didn't end there. I found that this lack of control went much deeper.

The human body is an amazing mix of flesh and bone, blood and juices all working together. If I were to look at myself under a microscope, I would see that my body reduces to chemicals, those chemicals reduce to compounds, and these compounds reduce to tiny molecules all dancing to the laws of motion. The most basic details about me—of my thoughts, my desires, my beliefs, my joys—were created by swirling masses of atoms slamming into one another. These explosions not only produced my fears and happiness and hopes and memories and pleasure and pain, they also produced my beliefs—my view of what was good, what was beautiful and what was true[2].

It got worse.

Without a God, I began to embrace the now clear fact that chemical events in my skull were creating what I called "love." Love wasn't really a decision or something mystical. "Love" was simply the way my biologically engineered brain responded when I was in the presence of a particular woman, and this extended to the rest of my family as well. The evolutionary success of my ancestors explained why I had such overwhelming feelings of care for my two boys. I love my boys immensely, but the philosophy I affirmed said that I have such feelings because the chemical reactions in my head say so—and tomorrow those chemicals might change direction.

It didn't stop. I know these chemicals would get hold of the commercials I watched, and they would determine what I wanted.

They got hold of the propaganda I read, and they would determine what I believed. Accidents and adrenaline decided my conflicts. Herd instinct and socialization determined my political beliefs. The activity in my temporal lobe produced my prior religious beliefs as well as all my new doubts. It seemed everything I thought, every act I performed, every desire I had, the entire course of my life could be explained by the forces within me over which I had no power. Einstein himself reached a similar point and said, "Thinking, feeling, and acting are not free but are just as casually bound as the stars in their motion."[3]

After stepping away from God, I began asking in a new way, "who am I?" and the very first thing that stood out was how little influence over my life I actually had.[4] Given my heritage and my biochemical make-up, I was no longer in the driver seat. Everything in me was steered by unthinking, unguided tornados of activity in my skull which began spinning long before I had any say in the matter. I could call it unacceptable, but *even the desire to rebel against the-chemical-reactions-which-control-me was itself a desire arising from the-chemical-reactions-which-controlled-me.* I might become a criminal; I might become a saint. Like a white knuckled four-year-old whose feet have slipped off the pedals, all I could do is watch and hope the results didn't hurt too much, because when I asked, "Why am I out of control? Why do I do the things I hate? Why can't I simply get my life together?" the answer was simple.

Sir Isaac Newton was making things fun.

THE SAME HOUSE

Such thoughts were depressing, and I'm not a depressed person. But I did want to be honest. I would be negligent if I didn't look coldly at what the sciences told me about myself and draw the right conclusions. I could assume that I was in complete command of my well-being, but of course the natural world painted clearly that such hopes were unsupportable. In fact, I knew it got much worse.

I realized this at my neighbor's house.

I seldom saw Bud, but I knew he had cancer. He lived next door to us with his wife Ingrid and rarely came outside. My boys and I first introduced ourselves when we went trick-or-treating last year. Bud opened the door in his bathrobe, a bowl of M&Ms in a large boney hand. He looked at the boys as they took the candies, stared up at me for a moment, and then backed into his home without a word. Bud was hospitalized shortly before Christmas and on New Year's Day he came home to die.

That night Ingrid came over to our house frantic.

It was warm for a January night, and I hurried behind her barefoot, crossed her lawn, and pushed open the front door. Bud and Ingrid's home had the same floor plan as ours and the same paint color. The only real difference was in the living room: where we have a coffee table, they had a large hospital bed. Bud was on the floor next to it, shaking and wearing only a diaper. Cancer had moved up into his brain and his system was filled with painkillers. He'd tried to get up a few minutes earlier when Ingrid was in the kitchen. He staggered, fell, and hit his face on the entertainment center next to the bed.

Ingrid and I lifted Bud back on the bedside. When we got him in place, Ingrid wiped the blood from his nose and lip with the cotton sheets. She laid Bud on his back, changed his large wet diaper, and sobbed. She didn't know what to do, and that made two of us. I gave her a hug, then she went to go call for help. Bud didn't want to stay down. He kept lurching forward, throwing his legs over the side of the bed, so I sat with my arm over his shoulder, keeping him stable, unaware that he would die in the next few hours. When I spoke to him, he didn't respond. Every few minutes he would try to stand and I would hold him closer. I told him Ingrid would be back soon. I told him everything would be okay. I told him I liked the paint color of his house.

Bud and I sat in that front room together a long time with nothing to do but stare at the shelves in front of us. Apparently he liked bird life and astronomy; many of his books were about the natural world. He also had a couple of books by some guy on the radio—political angst. But my eyes kept coming back to the center shelf and the picture in the brass frame. In it, Bud was standing with his arm around his daughter—the two of them smiling.

On that night in my neighbors' front room, I didn't just see another man die; I saw the future. My life may be enjoyable, at times even beautiful. I may accomplish all I wish. I may pursue and achieve "the good life", but the end has been scripted and it's not gracious. I will read my books, I will take my pictures, and then the world which handed me my out-of-control body will take it back again—and it will do so without thought or remorse.[5]

Again, I'm not a depressed person—and you may not be either—but I recognized that I was deceiving myself if I didn't play out the real and gripping consequences of death.

Everything around us is dying.

My wife will die. My sons will die. Everyone in my family will die. Everyone in my city and my culture will die. Everyone on this planet will die, and the human race fares no better. The earth will die when the sun grows to an enormous size and engulfs our world. Our solar system will die when the sun exhausts its remaining energy. Our galaxy of trillions of stars will eventually be gobbled up by another galaxy.[6] And the entire natural order will eventually die as our universe turns all its remaining gas into stars and those star inevitably burn out. Looking at a world like ours it is clear, *entropy holds the reigns*, and in the distant future all that will remain of our once beautiful cosmos will be a dark, thinning gas.[7]

On one front I thought, "Well, I might as well enjoy the ride while I can." But that didn't last long. I remember walking with a professor of mine, when this problem stood out to me with new clarity. We discussed how death was a thief, and it was robbing us now of all the significance, all the meaning we could hope to find. It struck me that everything I might want to build is already debris, for when I asked the question, "What should I do with my life? What should I care about?" there was only one answer available:

"It doesn't matter. Everything will evaporate."

Sure mature people will embrace their own mortality—but mere mortality was not what I found sickening. Once I acknowledged that nothing I did would last—that the only real value I experienced were times of pleasure when I was being productive or praised or delighted by a dinner with friends—then my anger truly took hold. These pleasures were the only points in my life I said, "had meaning." I could hold them up and say, "Well, it's not all that bad, at least I've got these moments." But this is where my struggle with death intensified, for I knew such blips of pleasure weren't significant at all. Pleasure was a chemical explosion in my skull.[8] The "meaning" I was holding up as so important, so worthy of all my attention and effort, was nothing more than fluids, luck, and the random collisions of molecules.

As I read it, this was the story the physical sciences told us, and it seemed clear to me that nothing I did would produce for me either a life of freedom or lasting significance. On the face of it, everything I cared about eventually reduced to chaos.

My journey back to belief in God began here. I consistently hit this spot where I had to recognize that the only hope for myself, my wife, my sons, my friends, or my culture to escape the ramifications of death and bondage to the chemicals within us was *help*—help from something immaterial, help from something separate from the blind, degenerating natural order. After the sciences have had their say and painted clearly our origin and our bio-chemical makeup, the overwhelming conclusion I hit over and again was that I required rescue. What other option is there? Yet the only thing that can rescue me is a supernatural being with both *the ability* to rescue me, and *the desire*.

And that sounded like a God to me.

If such a being does not exist, I thought, I will die like all other common things—and meaning, along with everything else I care for, will die with me.

NEGLIGENCE

I now teach courses about meaning and evil, justice and the good life, and I don't go into them without doubts or problems. I continue to ask myself about a world with and without a God. But each time that I re-up and ask what I hold as true—when I again pose the questions that will determine the kind of person I will become and what I will do with my life—these two observations are central: without something supernatural, I am just a chemical machine; without something supernatural, everything I care about will be erased.

Of course, you don't need to actually believe in God to see that a God is necessary for meaning, love, and freedom. Many of the wisest and most careful thinkers I know reject belief in God. They hold that life is absurd, yet many of them continue to look with hope—and this seems to me the most rational place to be.[9] Come down where you will, I find it ridiculous to pretend like God's existence makes no difference at all. Everything in my experience screams out that we should devote our best energies and thinking to looking, no matter how faint the hope.

Let me illustrate what I mean by that.

I transferred a utility bill six months ago when my family moved, but the power company did not transfer our service. When the new tenants began doing a major renovation in our old home, my family was paying for their electricity. I didn't realize the oversight because I'm allergic to small-print legalese and billing statements, but after a few months the power at our new home was cut off. I called the folks at the utility company. They told me the details of our account, and I thought, "Well, that's an easy fix." The company had made a mistake, and to resolve it they simply needed to transfer money we had already paid to the right account. Job done. The power company, however, had no record of my request to cancel service at my old home.

"It's not showing a record of your cancellation on my computer, sir," the man said.

"I realize it's not on your screen," I replied. "But I cancelled the account when I started service at my new home."

"Yes sir, but I don't have a record of your cancellation. It's just not on my screen, so I cannot refund your money."

"You're saying that if something is not on your screen, it didn't happen?"

"Yeah."

I didn't know that computer screens have the ability to alter historic facts, erase events, and change reality to serve the preferences of their corporate owner, but apparently they do.

This issue frustrated me for a week. Bring up the name of that power company and my body still gets tense and all those emotions take over any good mood I may be enjoying. Of course, I'm not unique. Our tempers can flair for hours when someone calls us a name, or our child spills a drink, or the neighbor's jukebox is still rocking at 3am. But what do we lose in such instances? Peace of mind, a few minutes cleaning the carpet, a night of restful sleep?

Still, such events have the power to dominate our thoughts. I remember specific times last year when my son spilled his juice, a night eight years ago when my neighbor's music was too loud, an unfortunate incident when I was seven and someone made fun of my clothes. (She was beautiful, she was popular, and the first time she spoke to me she said in a majestically conceited voice, "Seriously. You don't match.") In the big picture, these were minor irritants. None of them have had lasting value, but apparently I'm the kind of person that holds on to all sorts of totally insignificant events from my past as though they were the memory of my first kiss.

Now, imagine that you and I were informed that everything we own, everything we have built, every person we enjoy, every object of our affection will soon be destroyed with ruthless vigor right in front of us. Imagine that not a single thing we love will be spared. As opposed to shelling out a couple hundred bucks for a suspect electricity bill, the destruction of all we care for is worthy of our attention—but this is exactly what will happen!

The thoughtless natural order will eventually hack to pieces all those people and all those pleasures we love most. Such a future is not merely possible. It is scientifically verifiable.

It was when I reach this point—when I recognize that nothing in the natural world could make sense of meaning or freedom or the continuation of anything that I love—that I first begin to seriously look for a God again. This hasn't been a one-time epiphany for me. I come to this point of searching regularly. I recognize both in my mortality and my everyday struggles that hope requires *something* that can enliven my natural body—now, tomorrow, and into the future—and make my thinking, my feelings, my joys, sorrows, passions, and love supernatural. There's nothing any of us can do to create a lasting life or freedom. *We need a soul.* But no matter how hard we might look, nothing in the natural order can establish a soul. Evolution cannot provide us one. Apple won't be creating the iSoul. Only something of significant power can reach into our world from outside of nature and gift us a soul. Hope requires something beyond nature that not only has the power, but also has the will to breathe into us a bigger kind of life—a life of freedom, a life that lasts.

Eventually, I put it all together and I concluded that if love is real, if freedom is real, if lasting significance is possible then God must be real.[10] Only a God-like being could care about me and those I love. Only a God could choose to infuse us all with a life that is more than chemical reactions. Only a personality can see our natural plight, can understand that everything we build and every love we have is crumbling before us, only a being with considerable strength can see out situation and mercifully change our natural course. Death and genetics are immensely powerful, and I recognized that it would take something with enormous muscle and compassion to push back the course of nature so that everyone I care for might really live.

Perhaps you are different, but when I come to this point—the point at which I recognize that without help my life is unlivable—I realize I have every reason to look for something beyond this dying material world. I lose nothing by seeking a God who cares for me, but I will lose everything I care for if that God is not there.

NOTES

1   Richard Dawkins. *The Greatest Show on Earth: The Evidence for Evolution.* New York: Free Press, 2009.

2   I could take the argument further here and note that every belief I hold has been conditioned by my brain—a brain that evolved to this point not because it sought to discover truth, but because it's forbearers efficiently replicated DNA. Nothing more. Evolutionarily speaking, truth is not the natural target for brains. Reproduction, effective feeding, aggression, and defensiveness are. In fact, some beliefs—say, believing I will get brain cancer if I do not have a child with fifteen different partners this year, or believing that Zeus will strike me dead if I do not annihilate all my competitors—have *significant* evolutionary value. We could name many such beliefs that lead to effective reproduction and survival that are clearly false. And there's always the doubt that things I believe aren't really true. I believe them because of the evolutionarily predetermined movement of chemicals in my head.

3   Address to the Spinoza Society of America, September 22, 1932. (Quoted in "Einstein & Faith." Walter Isaacson. Time Magazine. April 5, 2007.) See http://bit.ly/agcOyU

4   In fact when I looked at my brain and body, it was hard to put my finger on "me."

5   Blaise Pascal, a writer who watched his own father die, said, "Imagine a number of men in chains, all under sentence of death, some of whom are each day butchered in the sight of the others; those remaining see their own condition in that of their fellows, and looking at each other with grief and despair await their turn. This is an image of the human condition." Pensees 199 (434), 1669

6   The Andromeda Galaxy is spinning toward us and in 3 to 5 billion years will engulf the Milky Way. Another new theory suggests the force of impact between the outer spirals of each galaxy will only minimally affect the gravitational balance until one of the super massive black holes at the center is close enough to eclipse the other—then all bets are off.

7   If the material world is all there is, it has a limited amount of potential energy and therefore there is no possible invention human ingenuity could create for itself to carry on indefinitely. Life is unsustainable in a universe like ours because it is a closed system. Just as our planet is running out of fossil fuels, so too the universe itself is using up all its potential energy. Because of entropy and the second law of thermodynamics, all matter is moving toward disorder, and as such the fuel upon which life depends must run out. Bertrand Russell, perhaps the greatest atheist thinker of the 20th century painted this well, writing, "All the labours of this age, all the devotion, all the inspiration, all the noonday brightness of human genius, are destined to extinction…the whole temple of Man's achievement must inevitably be buried beneath the debris of a universe in ruin." "*A Free Man's Worship*", 1903.

8   Conversely, my body could send up shrikes of pain at the sight of a sunset. It could give me a searing headache whenever I sit down with people I relate to. Meaning it seems is totally relative to the preconditions of my noetic make up, and my noetic make up was the result of chance.

9   As such Blaise Pascal rightly said, "The immortality of the soul is something of such vital importance to us, affecting us so deeply, that one must have lost all feeling not to care about knowing the facts of the matter. All our actions and thoughts must follow such different paths, according to whether there is hope of eternity or not, that the only possible way of acting with sense and judgment is to decide our course in the light of this point, which ought to be our ultimate objective. Thus our chief interest and chief duty is to seek enlightenment on this subject, on which all our conduct depends. *And that is why, among those who are not convinced, I make an absolute distinction between those who strive with all their might to learn and those who live without troubling themselves or thinking about it* … This negligence in a matter where they themselves, their eternity, their all are at stake, fills me more with irritation than pity; it astounds and appalls me; it seems to me quite monstrous" (Pensees 427. My emphasis).

10   If you need an argument for God's existence, you may be inclined to add an additional premise here based on your own intuitions: (2) Either love, freedom, or lasting significance is real. And therefore God is real.

Maybe I should say my prayers and light myself on fire,
And walk out on the wire once again.

Counting Crows
Good Night Elizabeth

2   GLASSES

My two boys have recently refused to eat anything but chicken nuggets. Not just any chicken nuggets, mind you. My 4 year old insists they be made by Tyson, shaped like dinosaurs, accompanied by both barbeque sauce and ketchup, and my 2 year old enthusiastically concurs. These dinosaur nuggets—alongside a multi-vitamin and vegetable juice—are often my boys' meal of choice for breakfast, lunch, and dinner. Our doctor says it's okay (apparently it's the calories that matter) and so my wife and I didn't worry about their eccentric food tastes until last week when every grocery store in our city ran out of dinosaur-shaped-Tyson-chicken-nuggets.

Perhaps your kids will eat something different after a few days of starvation, but apparently mine won't. We bought a variety of other nuggets, made by Tyson, made by McDonalds, made by the finest chefs on the planet—but none of these nuggets were acceptable. They were too small, too fancy. They were cut funny. They didn't look enough like a stegosaurus. Each time I served doppelganger nuggets, I would hear, "No, we want the dinosaur nuggets, daddy!"

"We don't have any dinosaur nuggets," I would explain. "But these are the same thing."

The boys argued that the dinosaur nuggets were hiding in the freezer, so I would show them the empty freezer.

"The dinosaur nuggets are at the store," they replied.

After several adventures to the frozen food isle, I would say, "Nope, no dinosaur nuggets at the store. Why don't you pick out some other nuggets?" But the boys wouldn't ask for new nuggets. They would ask for a new store—and by Day 3 of my kids not eating I was willing to take them.

Finally, on one of our trips back from a store in another town, we had a frank conversation about dinosaurs and extinction.

"It looks like you guys ate *all* the dinosaurs! They are all gone. The dinosaur nuggets are extinct."

They weren't convinced.

"Guys, I actually read in a book … um … that there was a huge meteorite that hit our planet a while ago and now there are no more dinosaurs … shaped like chicken nuggets … anywhere."

Which isn't quite a lie.

"That book is incorrect, daddy," my four year old said. "They are at a new store."

"No, it was written by a really smart guy from M.I.T."

"The dinosaur nuggets are at a *new* store."

To which the two year old began to chant, "New Sto! New Sto!"

"Seriously, guys, they're extinct. It's the dominant view of pale-ontologists everywhere."

Despite my best arguments, the chanting continued. Apparently, proving a universal negative to two persistent preschoolers can be quite difficult. In fact, it is difficult to show anyone who is filled with faith that the object of her faith does not exist. Those dino-saur nuggets could be hiding in a spot we haven't looked yet. They could be in a truck bound for the store we just left. They could be planning an invasion of our freezer with all their McNug-get buddies right now. The possibilities are endless.

My own experiments with agnosticism faced a similar problem. At the end of the day, there weren't any arguments that made God-belief mandatory. The arguments for God's existence were interesting and worthy of consideration, but I didn't think most of them proved what many thought they proved. I wasn't alone. I continue to see it every day—intelligent people who want God to exist but continue to think the reasons to believe fail. This is why many of my friends and colleagues see God-belief as goofy. They consider themselves thoughtful, educated people. They have looked at the physical evidence. They have considered the available proofs, and they do not find them compelling.

It seems to me, however, that lack of evidence isn't the real problem. The problem is how we choose to look at evidence. We often think that discovering whether or not God exists is like checking in the frozen food isle for dinosaur shaped nuggets. We think we should be able to detect God just like anything else.

This is an assumption, and this assumption is false.

Here's the thing about God—if a God exists, he is not just one among a wide swath of other facts in the universe. *God is a reality that colors and defines facthood.* If a God exists then the nature of our minds, the reliability of our brains, the function of reality itself—are each thoroughly affected. God is not just one among billions of other things that exist. God is a being whose creative influence and creative aims alter the light by which we understand our world and ourselves.

This is core for my own search for God. I left God belief when it was just about scanning the universe for a grey haired figure on his heavenly throne. But after walking away, it struck me over and over that if God is real, he is not simply a fact to be affirmed. God was a being who's light transformed the way I saw everything else.

In reconsidering the question, I found that God-belief was far more like the glasses through which we look at an empty freezer than the dinosaur nuggets we are searching for.

NOTE

Let me pause here and say this chapter won't be helpful for some of you.

I am going to display as quickly and cleanly as I can what it looked like for me to embrace *belief* in God. The previous chapter gave all kinds of emotional reasons for *wanting* a God to exist, and such arguments are good enough for many when they select (or de-select) their beliefs. But I'm a philosopher at heart, and I needed to go a bit further. Some of you will find this chapter unnecessary, like pausing to tell a friend how your eyes work before describing some captivating sight before you.

For me, understanding how God-belief works has been vital when looking for God. I couldn't move forward any other way. So if you find this chapter does not help you, does not meet you were you're at, do skip ahead.

For those of you who want to do some hard thinking—here we go.

NEW AND DIFFERENT THINGS

Seeing God-belief as a set of glasses wasn't that surprising. Much of the philosophy coming out in recent years shows us that *the way*[11] we look at the world influences and affects what we claim is true. That is, all "facts" are theory dependent. As such, the glasses we first decide to wear (or choose to change during the course of our lives) dictate what we believe is real.

Consider a recent example of how glasses work.

A hundred years ago photographs of a solar eclipse confirmed a new theory of the universe. The pictures were the first proof of Einstein's General Theory of Relativity as it replaced the classic

Newtonian view of absolute lines, absolute length, and absolute motion.[12] For a few dozen years, physicists knew that Newton's theories could not explain certain anomalies in nature, but they had no new theory that could. Such scientists knew they were seeing the world wrongly, but they could not adjust. With Einstein's Theory of Relativity, the scientific community was able to take off a set of glasses they had used for centuries and put on new ones that understood the entire physical order in a different way.[13] The perspective offered by Einstein changed the way a whole world saw our universe and our relationship to it.

Replacing inadequate glasses has taken place a few times in the history of science. Galileo's perspective made more sense of cosmology than Ptolemy's. Kepler's theories of motion replaced those of Aristotle. In each case, a revolution occurred when thinkers removed old theories like a deficient set of glasses and adopted new glasses that made better sense of the observed world. Historian of science Thomas Kuhn called the replacement of old glasses "paradigm shifts," and said, "When paradigms change, the world itself changes with them ... during revolutions scientists see new and different things when looking with familiar instruments in places they have looked before."[14]

Even in the physical sciences, a different perspective has the power to radically reshape the cosmos.

I find this picture helpful in understanding how you and I see God. We all have different experiences, different priorities, different hopes and desires. We all have different philosophies and paradigms that filter and color what we believe is real. We are all, it seems, wearing glasses—things we believe—that interpret and ground everything we hold as true. In order to affirm *anything*, we must begin by believing *some things* completely without evidence.[15]

In my own thoughts about God, I recognized that if I was going to talk about God at all, my conversation had to begin with my own glasses. My glasses were telling me who I was and what I could know. Reason was unable to provide "the right glasses," because my glasses told me what reason *was* and whether or not I should value it. This was not a chicken and the egg problem. I recognized that when I choose to believe in God and when I choose to disbelieve, I was selecting a pair of glasses and then seeing what those glasses told me to see.

EVERYONE LEAPS

At this point, I began to notice why, when I spoke about God as a believer and when I spoke about God as a skeptic, I was in essence describing two different worlds. When I choose to disbelieve in a God, I put on glasses through which no one could see a God. With such glasses in place, I was saying that *all facts* were assessed and understood through the physical sciences. Given such glasses, *of course* I would never see a non-physical, non-scientifically detectable being like God. *Of course* I would hold out hope for future scientific discoveries that make sense of the questions I knew science could not presently answer. "Evidence" wasn't the way I would discover God, for what I counted as evidence was being defined and interpreted by whichever possibility-determining, value-orienting, evidence-assessing glasses I selected for myself.

This presented a problem.

Because God-belief was a precondition for God-knowledge *both my belief in a God and the rejection of a God was initially a matter of my will, and not my intellect.* God-belief was something I was either going to assume at the beginning that allowed me to see God, or else God-belief was something I was going to reject at the outset making God invisible for the remainder of my life.

This problem of knowledge, philosophy, and God explained why so many of the intelligent people I knew on both sides of the debate about God held such vastly different opinions. In a world like ours it is clear that not everyone *wants* to begin with the same set of glasses. *Wants* differ from person to person.[16] Consider what Aldous Huxley, a brilliant and noteworthy atheist, said of his own quest,

> I had motives for not wanting the world to have a meaning; consequently assumed that it had none, and was able without any difficulty to find satisfying reasons for this assumption ... For myself, as no doubt for most of my contemporaries, [atheism] was essentially an instrument of liberation.[17]

What is praiseworthy in this quote is that Huxley—unlike many God-believers and fellow atheists—is honest enough to admit his glasses *were the result* of desire. Huxley affirmed that his own beliefs about what is real were motivated strictly by his passions.

Might this explain why brilliant men and women fall on both sides of the God question? Consider Blaise Pascal and Fredrick Nietzsche, Thomas Aquinas and David Hume, Polkinghorne and

Hawkings, Plantinga and Dennett—each pairing is surpassingly intelligent and each pairing comes to widely different conclusion on whether or not a God exists. On the face of it, such thinkers are not ignorant, wicked, or deceived (though it has become fashionable for both sides to claim so). These thinkers came to their beliefs honestly, and as such *intelligence does not lead toward or away from God-belief.* The intellect is initially impotent here.

I found that I agreed with Huxley. As I considered God again, I recognized that non-rational passions were selecting my glasses.[18] I saw myself, and thinkers much smarter than me, choosing to both wear the glasses that received a God and choosing the glasses that excluded a God. I was reminded of this tendency at a recent lunch.

A colleague of mine in philosophy, a man I consider a sage and whose insights and opinions I highly value, argued that God's existence is an affront to human freedom. If a God exists, he noted, this God would be aware of everything we do. God would be able to peer into our thoughts and minds without restraint—as such, God would be like the worst kind of tyrant.[19]

For my colleague, this was a deal killer, and I've seen other articulate atheists make the same claims.[20] Of course, this argument has nothing to do with whether or not a God actually exists. *This argument expresses a preference*, a preference to see the world without an omniscient being. And that is unavoidable, for both atheism and theism begin with such desires; they both begin with what we want.

I'm consistently convinced that belief in God begins with my heart and not with my head. It was this insight more than any others that allowed me to wrestle with the problem of evil.

WHY EVIL MOVED ME BACK TOWARD GOD

Anyone who thinks seriously about God has to think about the evil in our world—both the moral evils that some human beings inflict on others, and the natural evils that seem to unthinkingly strike even the best people.

When it came down to defending my agnosticism, this was the argument I offered. The suffering in our world gave me a good "reason" to reject God-belief, for certainly a good God would act decisively to end sex slavery. A good God would destroy Malaria. A good God would not remain silent in the face of war, disease, the death of children, and the other tragedies that countless millions experience each day. As such, I found tragedy and wickedness good motives for doubting God's existence.

It was an honest move to say, "I don't believe in God because of pain," but in retrospect I was kidding myself if I thought it was an intellectual move. Reason had nothing to do with it. When I was self-critical, my cold skepticism could kill the problem of evil and suffering quickly.[21]

It *could be* the case that every innocent person who suffers will derive immense, life-transformative value from their suffering if God is real and their lives extend beyond death.[22] It *could be* the case that everyone who suffers—whether they are a two-year-old who starves to death, a middle age man with brain cancer, or the victim of a ghastly rape and murder—will in God's future look on such events as deeply meaningful and even necessary. They might even insist to you and me in some future conversation that their pain was a treasure, and that I insult them by degrading their pain as "meaningless."[23] *I just couldn't know!* Because of my limited knowledge—rationally—I had to remain skeptical.[24]

Today I am watching a friend of mine who is not yet thirty wrestle with lung cancer. I have had friends die in car wrecks. I got an email last night from a couple who are not yet 20 but are struggling in the aftermath of finding a large lump in her right breast. I make it a point to read about the warfare, genocides, and mass-starvation presently taking place in our world. I am fully aware of natural disasters that devastate whole regions, the wake of destruction left by AIDS, and the artistic violence some people perpetrate on the innocent. These details of our world are clearly on my radar. Yet these are events, like all other events, whose meaning and significance become apparent only after interpretation by my glasses, and they must be interpreted through yours as well.

The best arguments I discovered both for and against God's existence—the ones I found most persuasive—really weren't "reasons" at all. They were appeals to my emotions, and this makes sense because when it came down to it, emotions selected my glasses. At the end of the day, desire decided whether I believed in a God or not. My desire for meaning and my lack of freedom were good reasons to re-consider God, *but I took off the agnostic glasses and replaced them with God-belief because of evil.* This move was an emotional decision to be sure, but this was a new and decisive point on my path back to God belief.

Here's how it worked.

When I assumed that there was no God, the value and meaning of suffering in our world was fairly clear. As many have pointed out, in a universe of blind physical forces some people will get hurt, other people will get lucky, and we won't find any rhyme or reason in any of it.[25] When I put on the "No-God" glasses, it seemed clear to me that the vast majority of horrific suffering failed to lead to *any* identifiable good. Most tragedies kill the victim before the victim can find any meaning in their pain. As such, when a young girl dies of bone cancer, when a region is drowned by a tsunami, when a man detonates a bomb laced with nails and ball bearings in a crowded area—these catastrophes have no resolution. They just are. If there was no God, I thought, such victims couldn't experience their pains being made right again, couldn't work through the tragedy to find some value. Such evils were just a brute fact to swallow at gravesites.

Conversely, if God was real, suffering and death might be doors leading to new lands. They might be experiences that eventually had some purpose, for no matter what might happen to the body of someone suffering, her soul might grow, her mind might progress, her future self that God was presently fashioning might transform into something far more substantial. When I looked at a desperately sad event through these two sets of glasses—those that acknowledged and those that denied God's reality—only one held out the potential for real hope. The other was irredeemably tragic.

Suffering gave me a substantial reason to try the God-belief glasses back on, for a God alone could take a world that was clearly decaying and transform those spots into something alive. But unless I first believed I would not see God—and if there was no God, most of the pain experienced by those I love, by most of humanity in fact, was plainly pointless.

Really believing that there is a God and acting like it—began here.

If I choose to believe in a God and he didn't exist, I lost nothing. God was just another set of glasses worth trying. But if there was a God and I failed to seek him, I might lose everything. I would have willingly chosen to view the world as though what was ultimate was an illusion. I would have failed to connect myself—my body, mind and soul—to the only everlasting reality.

Yes, searching for a God was a risk. It was a path that might end with the painful silence of a void. But I would not find God if I continued to choose glasses that excluded him. In order to see God, I had to remove my agnostic glasses, set them aside, and put on a set that assumed some rationality guided the world around me, that even the most heart-breaking pains and tragedies in our world might be transformed someday into a bigger good.

That's a much larger exploration, one we will take up shortly, but the path needed to start with a leap back into God belief. Instead of seeing the world as though it was all random, I began by *assuming* that my life and the lives of those around me were made for a good reason. The easiest way to do this was to simply speak to God again, to treat God as though he had been there all along.

The best thing I did at this point was to simply begin saying, "thanks"—thanking God for the things I enjoyed most, for the people I loved, even for the small things that went right. This step more than any other allowed me to see the world not as chaos but as *telos*—as a painting, as a work of art made with intention. Thanks awakened me to rhythms and realities I would not have been aware of before.[26]

I took this step because remaining in a godless world was so obviously repugnant. If God was absent then our lives, with all the spots of light in them, were surrounded by darkness, but if God was real then our lives, with all the spots of darkness in them were surrounded by light.[27]

WORDS

At the end of a semester after all the papers are in and grades are done, I take my students out for pizza at the pub across the street for our "final." That story has gotten out, and I now have no trouble filling my classes.

Last semester, I had just one student over the age of twenty-five. He was a strong man, very intelligent, and had just finished his time overseas in Iraq. Near the end of the year a friend of his, who had returned with him from the war, committed suicide. My student skipped some of the classes to go the funeral, and I hadn't spoken to him since he got back, but he came out to the pub for the final. The other students left one by one to prepare for other tests that week, but we stayed late, talking about all kinds of things. After one too many beers and a discussion on politics and events happening in the Middle East, he got quiet and said, "Imagine you're walking down an alley. And you've got a job to do. And a twelve year old jumps out in front of you with a gun ... You shoot right?"

Most people aren't malicious. They don't desire the destruction of others, but they find themselves doing things that are deeply troubling. That night the only place my student had to turn to address his past—to wrestle with his own demons and suicidal thoughts, to ask if he was somehow in the right or if he was just another killer—was to the philosophy teacher who mentions Jesus sometimes. But what he needed most at that moment—more than a justification for his actions or somebody telling him that he was okay—was someone to repair his past. He needed someone to make a bad situation right again.

This is God's job. If the God we are looking for exists, we must ask what tangible, decisive actions he is pursuing *now* to rescue his world. Because God is supremely loving and gracious, he must be doing something to address the suffering many of us experience. In fact, if God exists, perhaps it is in the suffering, in the hardship, in the places of trial and heartache, that we will see him most clearly.

There's an ancient poem of God creating our world that provides a clue.

In this story, God hovers over chaotic waters. The raw material God sees is dark and formless. In the beginning it seems nothing was good or beautiful, nothing was wisely orchestrated. It was all confused.[28] Then the God said, "Let there be light," and what was once in disarray suddenly reconstructed around the words of God. There was renewal and purpose. God took what was once unstable and from it made a new home for humanity and himself. Out of what was unsettled and ugly, God crafted a new creation.

The Hebrew culture was one of the earliest God-belief cultures, and they often pictured God's orchestrating power in personal terms, saying things like,

To you, O people, I call out;
I raise my voice to all humankind …
Listen to my instruction and be wise;
Do not disregard it.
Blessed are those who listen to me,
Watching daily at my doors,
Waiting at my doorway.
For those who find me find life.[29]

Such pictures show God's wisdom as not simply a principle or unconscious form. God's wisdom has a personality. Wisdom itself is passionate about the lives of mere human beings—pursuing them, speaking to them, showing them the beauty of a life in tune with reality.

Of course, the Jews were not unique. The Greeks embodied Wisdom in the figure of Metis, the spouse of Zeus who was one of the Titans. The Egyptians had Saa, the god of wisdom pictured with papyrus in hand. The Norse affirmed Odin, the Sumerians Enki symbolized by the early Capricorn. In each case, the ancients pictured Wisdom as an otherworldly reality. Such gods spoke through prophets or oracles, in divinations or signs. Wisdom was audible, but lacked physicality, so the proponents of these gods constructed idols, statutes and hieroglyphics to display wisdom—to bring it closer.

In a set of writings from the first century, a group of common middle easterners spoke of wisdom. But they pointed at a man—at a flesh and blood person. The man they encountered went around acting like the creator, reordering what was unstable, bringing health to dark lives and dysfunctional bodies. It was as though the God who once spoke over chaos was speaking again right in front of them. These first century Jews saw evil as a clue to where they would find God, for if a God was real he would not only care about the poor, the sick, and the broken. He would act on that care: feeding them, mending them, and raising them up again.

In this man the ancient portrait of wisdom, the defeat of evil, and the remaking of a world gone wrong all came together. This man had a unique ability to set right not only the physical world, but also systematic injustice and the dark pursuits of the human heart. Here it seemed God was speaking again over a world in disarray. Here wisdom was active, no longer incorporeal but present with us in the darkness, speaking in its own voice, renewing the world it loved, binding up what had been shattered, and releasing it all toward a day of total renewal. This man astonished everyone who heard and saw him.

And this man was Jesus.

NOTES

11   As a related point for those interested in the Bible, consider how the early Christians used the Greek Hodos, commonly translated "the Way" (specifically as the understanding of their own faith/point of view/glasses/ perspective in such passages as Acts 9:2, 19:9, 19:23, 22:4 24:22 (among others). Pair that with how they use Hodos in reference to the kind of path they journeyed upon: Mark 10:46-52 (v. 52 "the road" = Hodos), Matthew 7:13-14, (again "the road" = Hodos), John 14:4-6, et al). It may be that much contemporary philosophy is just restating what was assumed long ago.

12   Paul Johnson. Modern Times. (New York: Harper Perennial, 1992.) 1. The solar eclipse showed that a ray of light just grazing the surface of the sun bent by twice the amount provided for by the classical Newtonian theory. This observation was the first of three which would suggest Einstein's theory had more explanatory power than Newton's.

13   And of course Einstein's theories may be overtaken sometime in the future as well. Einstein himself spent the majority of his life trying to refute the indeterminacy principle of quantum mechanics, seeking to anchor physics in a unified field theory (Johnson, 4). If a later physicist succeeds in such work it may require striping away general relativity and replacing it with a fundamentally new perspective.

14   Thomas Kuhn. The Structure of Scientific Revolutions. Third Edition. (The University of Chicago Press: Chicago, 1996) 111.

15   For example, most of us believe—totally without evidence—that our brains are reliable. Nothing we do can prove the reliability of our brains. Any evidence we might cite to prove that our brains are reliable would be analyzed, affirmed, and given value by the very brain we are trying to show trustworthy. So, too, we believe without evidence that we are not a brain in a jar dreaming away. We believe without evidence that those we love have a mind like ours and are cognitively aware as we are. We believe without evidence that the future will be like the past. We believe without evidence that there is a physical world all around us—for everything we see, taste, and touch could be an illusion. We might add to this substance and causation as Hume did, or time as Kant did. Notice that causation, time, and experience of the external world are the foundation of the natural sciences. Thus, as I will argue later, any truth suggested by naturalism is grounded upon assumptions. "Yeah," someone might say, "but everyone believes those sorts of things." And this is certainly true if you believe there is a physical world around you, if you believe it is populated with people who have beliefs like yours, if you believe that you can know about the world around you with your suspect brain. If we are self-critical, it seems we believe all kinds of things without evidence. And these beliefs are the glasses through which we see the world. Such assumptions are unavoidable—for knowledge of our world has to begin with something, and since it cannot begin with things that are proved, it must begin with things that are believed. And if you are like me, you want there to be a physical world that can be understood. You want other people to have a mind like yours. You want to have a real past. You want your brain to be reliable, and you don't want to be a brain in a jar because you want your experiences to be real. It seems that when we begin to believe things, we start by believing what we want to believe. This is not bad. Unless we're masochists, it is difficult to see how we could do otherwise.

16   For example, one tradition begins by saying that everything we experience is mental. That we never actually encounter or enjoy a world "out there," that all we know are the mental events going on in our minds. Given this set of glasses, understanding what the mind is doing is the first and most vital step to understanding everything else. Another tradition begins by suggesting that the physical world is "all there is, or ever was, or ever will be," that everything can be understood materially, and that there are no such things as minds. Given this set of glasses, all truth will be discovered through our five senses and as such an exclusive commitment to the scientific method is the most vital step to understanding everything else. Another tradition begins with the belief that we are each a piece of a single cosmic reality. "Everything is one," they may say, and as such believing that "I" exist is a misstep. On this belief, the one thing you are not is an "I." You are part of the larger interconnected reality.

Given this set of glasses, transcending yourself as a thinking thing is the first and most vital step to understanding everything else. And some believe we are more than a physical brain—that though we are part of the material world, our minds are free and reliable because a God has created them free and reliable. Because we were fashioned by a being with understanding and intention, we can trust the reliability of our brains and the world around us. Given this set of glasses, affirming a design and proper function to our thinking is the first and most vital step to understanding everything else. These are four popular sets of glasses through which we might see and interpret reality. Commonly called Idealism, Materialism, Monism, and the later a blend of theism and metaphysical dualism.

17   Aldous Huxley. Ends and Means: An Inquiry into the Nature of Ideals and into the Methods Employed for Their Realization (Santa Barbara: Greenwood Pub Group, 1969) 269-270, 273. The fuller quote says, "The philosopher who finds no meaning in the world is not concerned exclusively with a problem in metaphysics, he is also concerned to prove that there is no valid reason why he personally should not do as he wants to do, or why his friends should not seize political power and govern in the way that they find most advantageous to themselves. For myself, as no doubt for most of my contemporaries, the philosophy of meaningless was essentially an instrument of liberation. The liberation we desired was simultaneously liberation from a certain political and economic system and liberation from a certain system of morality … The supporters of these systems claimed that in some way they embodied the meaning (a Christian meaning, they insisted) of the world. There was one admirably simple method of confuting these people…we could deny that the world had any meaning whatsoever."

18   In the Christian tradition the selection of glasses that see reality in a specific way is often called "faith"—and no matter what glasses you choose, it is unavoidable.

19   He similarly argued another emotion-driven reason based on the fact that the lover metaphor often used to describe our connection to God wasn't appealing, for he saw God as male and was himself heterosexual; nor was the

father metaphor appealing because he had not had a good experience with his own father, and the idea of getting another one was not all that desirable.

20   Nietzsche makes this point, and I heard Christopher Hitchens recently advance this argument though I do not know if it is any of his books on God. ("Does the God of Christianity Exist, And What Difference Does it Make?" Christianity Today Podcast. 4.16.2009 or http://blog.christianityto-day.com/ctliveblog/archives/2009/04/does_the_god_of.html)

21   A distinction here is critical. This argument targets the logical problem of evil. The logical problem of evil suggests that it must be the case that, given the amount and quality of evil in our world, God does not exist. I think it fair to say that most philosophers think that the "logical problem of evil" fails. There are too many possible outs. The argument that is advanced most often by professional thinkers here is what is often called "the evidential problem of evil" which suggests that innocent suffering makes the existence of a God less likely.

22   An afterlife is a common aspect of most forms of theism and is not an ad hoc addition here.

23   As Ivan Karamazov argues, "Suppose I suffer intensely. No one else can ever know how much I suffer, because he is another and not I." (Fyodor Dostoyevsky. The Brothers Karamazov. 1898).

24   Of course, it can go further. Suffering is seen as a reason to reject god-belief not because it is painful, but because it is seen as meaningless. Most of us choose to endure meaningful pain like root canals, or childbirth, or marathons. As such suffering itself is not a sufficient disproof of God, if that suffering has meaning. But notice, you and I cannot judge the meaning of someone else's pain. We do not have that ability. An unbridgeable cognitive distance exists here, for meaning is not assessed from a third person vantage point. As such, we cannot paint with a broad brush the apparent lack of meaning in events even like the holocaust or the many who live with debilitating ailments—unless such pains are our own. Nor do we see what such pains—even those resulting in death—will accomplish in the lives of those who suffer. For if our lives continue on after death, even the most horrific suffering may be assessed by the victim as surpassingly valuable. And what would our limited opinion mean if, say, the holocaust victim, 10,000 years into God's future, said that event was the soil in which the beauty of her soul grew. What could we possibly say to that, if she embraced such pain as instrumentally good? As it stands we ought to be very skeptical when looking at an event and saying, "That clearly has no purpose or value." If we are rational, it seems we are unable to make such assessments.

25   Richard Dawkins. *"God's Utility Function,"* Scientific American, November 1995, p. 85

26   On thanks. When I said thanks, sometimes it seemed that God was a distant listener, and that was okay. Sometimes a silent listener is the best kind. Other times I actually felt as though God was close, perhaps even wishing my best. Other times I sensed God inside me, sometimes prompting me to say certain things, sometimes encouraging me to go forward. Saying thanks wasn't so much about communication as much as it was about lining up my own heart and mind with a new reality.

27   See Peter Kreeft. Fundamentals of the Faith. (San Francisco: Ignatius, 1988) 119-120.

28   Genesis 1:2

29   Proverbs 8:1,4,32-35

PART TWO AND GOD SAID

I have seen the flaming swords there over east of Eden
Burning in the eyes of the maker

Daniel Lanois
The Maker

3   BILLBOARDS

Whenever I look for a God, I encounter Jesus.

Many of my friends will tease that when I believe, all I am doing is putting faith in an ancient book, but of course that's not how I get there. When I scan the philosophies about God, when I look for a narrative driving history, when I encounter a personality in my prayers, when I simply ask, "If there was a God what would it look like?"—they move me toward Jesus. I'm not the first by any means. Many people—educated and ignorant, wealthy and destitute, from countless generations and hyper-diverse cultures—have found that in this man God becomes tangible.

My own step toward Jesus didn't hinge on a bunch of religious experiences. I moved back toward Jesus when I studied, really for the first time, his personality—his magnetically keen personality. That was the move for me. There are many places I might point, but Jesus' personality is the place I see God most clearly. And I find I not only say, "Yes, this God is real," but better still, "I want this God to be real."

That's where my path has taken me; that's where my commitment now lies, and it happens still. Whenever I look for God, I consistently encounter Jesus. He is the personality at the other end of prayers, both those answered and those denied. He is the one who speaks unexpectedly. I have no trouble painting a picture of God in my mind because the deity I sense orchestrating the world around me and inviting me to jump in so often looks like this man. I find my steps toward Jesus a strange, unexpected path, sometimes a hard path. But on that road—when I hear Jesus' voice from distant times and look at his actions with fresh eyes—I am compelled again that this is the God I have been looking for.

And this is what I see.

REPAIR

Jesus was born to a poor family who lived in the hill country of northern Israel at the beginning of the Common Era. Jesus' father worked as a hired hand because his family owned no land, and hence had no wealth. Jesus' family was devoutly Jewish, living in Israel during a time when the Roman Empire occupied their country and used much of the local wealth to fund Rome's global expansion. Jesus was the firstborn, so when his father died Jesus helped care for his mother and her other children until his mid-30s.[30] As such, Jesus' early life was that of the common poor—working hard to survive in a land pillaged by the local elite and distant kings.

Despite these limitations, Jesus was a brilliant man. It is argu-able that no other thinker—ancient or modern—has had a better understanding of the human person than Jesus of Nazareth.

Any fool can write volumes upon volumes about the human con-dition if afforded the time. True genius speaks through simplicity. Note just one example of Jesus' insight and awareness. Early in his career, Jesus paired a core human psychology, normative ethic, national identity, and legal theory with a revolutionary the-ology in an easily memorized, action focused teaching. Today, we call this teaching the Sermon on the Mount. Given its cross-cultural power and short duration, the Sermon on the Mount holds up against any other intellectual achievement. Plato's *Republic*, Aristotle's *Nicomachean Ethics*, Kant's *Groundwork of the Metaphysics of Morals*, and David Hume's *An Enquiry Concerning the Principle of Morals*–arguably the greatest works on ethics in the western philosophical tradition—added together have not changed so many lives nor stimulated as much thought as this single address.

And it's just one of Jesus' teachings.

We should assume that Jesus' education was ordinary—that he learned from his parents and local teachers.[31] Like all other Jewish men his age, Jesus went three times a year to the fes-tivals in Jerusalem some 60 miles away from his home, where he dialogued with the great thinkers of his day.[32] Jesus memo-rized large portions of the Jewish scriptures. In fact, by the time he was thirty, Jesus had mastered the themes and underlying currents of the Jewish holy books. He had creatively wrestled with these texts, producing innovative interpretation which took both the Jewish story and ethical thought to profound, eventually world-changing heights.

Then, around the age of 34, Jesus started a revolution.

Collecting followers, Jesus began his uprising by teaching in the small towns and fishing villages of northern Israel where he made his home.[33] In fact, he did not teach in the large cities of Israel until the last week of his life.[34] Still, Jesus quickly developed a reputation—one so powerful that some men left their futures and family not simply to learn from him, but to revolt against the political and religious systems at work in their country and in their world.

Of course, being a revolutionary is not unique. But Jesus was exceptional in his personal charisma, his non-violent methods, and in the unique signs through which he communicated—signs that today all but the most skeptical scholars regard as, in principle, historical.[35] If one divorces Jesus from his recorded miracles, one quickly loses Jesus, for his signs are interlocked with most of his teachings, most of his activities, and were the obvious reason for his popularity. Without such signs, we are left with a Jesus who didn't do or say much, and as such wouldn't have developed a following large enough to provoke local authorities or warrant his well-documented execution.

Clearly then, Jesus did perform what his contemporaries saw as signs, and these signs were key to his message. Jesus acted and then challenged his followers and his culture to figure out the meaning of his actions. Early on his reputation for unique exhibitions of power pushed Jesus and his followers out of the small towns and into the countryside where thousands, sometimes tens of thousands, traveled to hear him speak—many hoping that he would touch them or a sick relative.

Now, the focus of Jesus' signs was quite specific. In his acts one sees the physical world, the mental world, the world of the soul and society all being *repaired*. When Jesus prayed for the broken, they stood. When he summoned the dead, they responded. When he spoke to storms, they stopped. When Jesus acted realities that had been out of tune suddenly harmonized, for Jesus was not simply a good teacher; Jesus was a conscious imitator of the creator. Jesus spoke over a world in disarray and began reconstructing what was once chaotic.[36]

Consider one of many possible examples: Jesus began the last week of his life with a miracle. He stood above a blind man and invited him to see. This miracle set in motion what many call "Holy Week," the six days moving from Palm Sunday to Good Friday. Jesus' symbolism was intentional. Just as God had spent six days making the cosmos, so at the beginning of his final six days of work Jesus chose to hover over darkness and, in essence, say to a blind man: let there be light. Jesus' biographer Mark didn't miss the ancient imagery. In describing the end of that day, Mark copied the poem of creation in Genesis and said, there was evening (Mark 11:11) and there was morning (Mark 11:12)—the first day of a new creation event.[37]

The healing of this blind man is an example of how Jesus used his signs. Jesus was never concerned with showcasing his power. He never turned his enemies into toads or moved a boulder into the air with his mind. Instead, Jesus' miracles communicated information. Notice the pattern: Jesus healed the sick, the paralyzed, and those whose hands didn't work as they should.[38] He made the deaf hear, the mute speak, and the blind see.[39] Jesus cured diseases like leprosy and hemorrhaging that kept human beings ostracized and separated from their families.[40] He repaired works of violence.[41] Jesus transformed the psychology of otherwise healthy human beings compelled to destroy themselves, and cast away powers that left some in mental slavery.[42] In his most dramatic signs, Jesus fed the starving masses, quieted storms, and raised two dead children and one man to life days after they had died.[43] *These are each acts in which God's creation had gone wrong, and Jesus set it right.* Jesus did not scrap the old and create something else in its place. Nearly all Jesus' miracles were acts of reversal—taking what was dysfunctional and returning it to health and symmetry.

At one point, when picturing for his followers where God was taking his world, Jesus spoke of the "the renewal of all things."[44] The phrase is actually a single Greek word, *palingenesia*. *Palin* means "second" or "repeated," and *genesia* is literally the word "birthday." But in Jesus' culture, as in our own, "Genesis" referred also to God creating the world out of the chaos.[45]

Jesus' anticipation of renewal was not unique. Most of Jesus' contemporaries believed that God would eventually act in a decisive way to eliminate evil and launch a new age in which God's will was done on earth as it was in heaven. Jesus frequently called this the "age to come",[46] and when he unpacked what his miracles meant, Jesus pictured our world moving toward that new birth. Jesus believed God would act decisively and institute a new day in which death and dysfunction no longer prevailed. God would pull all creation into a new period characterized by the recreation of everything that was confused and mangled. Jesus believed that heaven would not stand far off, but heaven—the presence and reconstructive authority of God—would descend and wed itself to this world which had for too long been corroding away. But the renewal of all things was not a distant vision for

Jesus. Jesus believed the restoration had begun in his actions and in the work of those who would follow him.

Jesus began his public career by simply announcing, "The time has come! The Kingdom of God is arriving!"[47] Jesus characterized God's renewal of all things like a train whose horn we hear, whose smoke we see, whose vibrations we feel as it pulls into the station. Jesus believed God's restructuring of every spoiled place was finally in sight and in small pockets—most obviously in the miracles he performed on God's behalf—this renewal was becoming a reality.[48] The shattered creation, too long neglected, was beginning to be put back together again through Jesus' own actions and soul-restoring truths.

Any time Jesus spoke of God's rule and presence, Jesus referred to it as "heaven,"[49] and because he thought heaven had come near, he taught his followers how to embrace it.

RISE

Jesus told a story about a man and his lost son. The boy had deeply insulted his father and moved to a distant country where he wrecked his life. After many months, broken and starved, "he got up" and went to his father. The father had been waiting, each day staring off at the distant road. When he saw his son, the old man ran out to meet him. He clutched the boy to his chest, called for a feast, and celebrated that "this son of mine was dead and is alive again."[50]

The picture is of a resurrection. The picture is of heaven running out to envelop the dead. This is Jesus' picture of God. He is not a distant deity. This God scans the horizon for people who maim themselves, who trash others, who waste his gifts, who find themselves starved and desperate for their lives to be put right. This God loves to find dysfunctional humanity, and this God runs out to meet them—to restore them to himself, to call them sons and daughters again, to remove the garments they have soiled and dress them in fresh clothing. When this God sees a dead child, he apparently will not leave them in a tomb. Jesus' God loves to resurrect the dead.

Entering dark places and raising human beings to a new kind of life was Jesus' primary activity. "They got up" is the most common description of those who encountered Jesus. It happens at least twenty times in the short narratives we have of Jesus' life. Consider just the stories written by Mark, the first biographer of Jesus.

In the first chapter of Mark's story, Jesus entered the home of a friend whose mother-in-law was sick with a lethal fever. "[Jesus] went to her, took her hand, and helped her *up*." In the second chapter, Jesus walked down an ancient highway and approached a tollbooth. The man there was a Levite—one of the priestly class—who had sold out to the Roman authorities and was now extorting money from his countrymen. Jesus looked at the man and said, "Follow me." And the tax collector "*got up*." In the third chapter of Mark, Jesus entered a synagogue and he saw a man with a deformed hand. Again Jesus said, "*Stand up* in front of everyone" and the man was healed. In the fourth chapter, it is Jesus himself who "*gets up*" from the stern of a boat to quiet a storm. In chapter five, Jesus raised a dead twelve-year-old to life again with the words, "I say to you, *get up!*" In chapter six, people from all over his country began carrying the sick *on mats* so they might lay their loved ones in front of Jesus. Mark says,

"All who touched him were healed,"[51] rising from their mats and walking home. In chapter nine, Jesus commanded an evil spirit from a child, leaving the boy pale and motionless. Those around said of the boy, "He's dead." "But Jesus took him by the hand and lifted him to his feet, and he *stood up*." In chapter ten, Jesus calls out to a blind man who is sitting by the road asking travelers to give him a gift. "Throwing his cloak aside [along with all the money he had collected,] the blind man *jumped to his feet* and came to Jesus" and received his sight.

And on and on.

The stories and teachings of Jesus are all deconstructions of what he was doing; and what he was doing was raising people from dead, dehumanizing conditions.

Resurrection is at the heart not only of the vast majority of Jesus' signs but also of his political teachings. The Sermon on the Mount, for example, begins with a portrait of the poor in spirit, the meek, the mourning, those hungering for their lives to be put right, being raised into a new kind of life—an identity as the light of the world, the salt of the earth, a new home for God like Jerusalem, the city on a hill. The Sermon ends with a picture of two men building homes: one that falls with a great crash and one that stands. The image is again of a temple, one built on Jesus' words rising and one that rejects his words falling.[52]

The trend continues. The image of resurrection is the central image of many of Jesus' stories as well.[53] In his first and most important parable, Jesus pictured a farmer in a rotten field,

> As [the farmer] was scattering the seed, some fell along the path, and the birds came and ate it up.

Some fell on rocky places, where it did not have much soil. It sprang up quickly, because the soil was shallow. But when the sun came up, the plants were scorched, and they withered because they had no root. Other seed fell among thorns, which grew up and choked the plants, so that they did not bear grain. Still other seed fell on good soil. It came up, grew and produced a crop, some multiplying thirty, some sixty, some a hundred times.[54]

I planted two tomato plants in our small garden this year. If I had a hundred fold increase, everything in my yard would be packed and overflowing with tomatoes. That's the picture here. This farmer entered a garden that had been neglected, a place life found it difficult to grow and enemies worked against a thriving crop—but when the farmer's seed took root, all the space that was once formless and void jammed with the fruit the farmer chose to plant.

What then was this seed that was doing such work? Jesus tells us later that the seed is "God's word"—what God is saying. This image takes us back again to Genesis. The Bible begins with God speaking over a garden, and this vocal act fills the earth.

The Lord God had planted a garden in the east, in Eden; and there he put the man he had formed, God created human beings in his own image, ...and God blessed them and said to them, "Be fruitful and increase in number; fill the earth."

"Fill the earth" is the first command given by God to humanity in the[55] scriptures. Likewise, Jesus' story of the farmer was about

God speaking again over his world, and picturing its resurrection from a dead garden into one raised to new life.

The parable is significant because Jesus saw himself as the farmer, walking through the garden filled with thorns, scorching heat, and rocky soil. He was the one planting new seeds in good soil that would be fruitful and multiply,[56] that would fill the earth, and that would transform everything in a creation too long overrun by weeds and thorns. The parable points to Jesus' own self-understanding. In his work, Jesus saw the creator God remaking the world around him. Thus, Jesus began using titles for himself that pictured himself as the truth God spoke,[57] or as the temple where humanity would meet God,[58] or as "the Son of Man", Jesus' favorite self-description, a divine portrait from the Jewish scriptures of one who would set the world right and inaugurate God's kingdom.

As in so many of his teachings, Jesus emphasized the point of his farmer story with a miracle latter that night.

STORM

When evening came, Jesus led his students to the Sea of Galilee near his hometown and said to his followers, "Let us go over to the other side."[60] They all got in a boat and halfway across an intense storm hit them. Waves broke over the boat so that it was nearly swamped, but Jesus didn't help. He was sleeping in the stern on a cushion. The disciples woke him and said to him, "Teacher, don't you care if we drown?" The writer tells us Jesus got up, rebuked the wind, and said to the waves, "Quiet! Be still!" Then the wind died down and it was completely calm.[61]

Like Jesus' other signs, this miracle was not simply an exhibition of power. Building on the story of the farmer told earlier that day, this miracle at sea pointed back to Genesis,

> "In the beginning God created the heavens and the earth. Now the earth was formless and empty, darkness was over the surface of the deep, and the Spirit of God was hovering over the waters." And God said, "Let there be light."[62]

The very first line of the Bible has God above dark waters, and speaking. Here, standing in the back of a boat, as terrified men and women call out to God for help, Jesus rose up and, hovering over dark water, he said, "Be still!"[63]

Notice how similar this story of Jesus calming the sea is to the story of the farmer. In both of them, things have gone wrong. There is opposition—storms, trials, hardship—and then God begins to speak. His word begins to go out, and what happens when God speaks? Barren places fill with fruit. Natural evils are overrun. The creator brings harmony to what was once out of control.

More interesting still is how Jesus reordered the chaos. A storm raged while Jesus lay down, *then he got up* and spoke. This is an essential detail. Mark, the author here, reminds us later that Jesus laid down at another significant time.[64] After his crucifixion, Jesus was laid in a tomb, but early on Sunday morning—after the Sabbath day celebrating God's rest—Jesus got up.

Mark used the image of resurrection throughout his telling of Jesus' story because he wanted us to see that Jesus' resurrection was not simply a display of power. The resurrection of Jesus was how God spoke again over a world in chaos. *Mark thinks Jesus, through his resurrection, started the palingenesia—*the renewal of all things. Jesus is the seed planted which rises and spreads its life into a barren world too long over run with dysfunction and death. The resurrection is how God responds to shouts of help from human beings all destined to die. The resurrection is how God produces a new kind of life that will eventually consume all of creation.

THE PROBLEM AT HAND

Though Jesus' resurrection is the most controversial aspect of his life, I have found it worthy of my consideration. Again, I am not interested in looking at the world anymore as mere nature. I am looking for a God to act, and all the signs come together for me here.

When I consider my own condition, my helplessness without something supernatural to rescue me, when I consider the dysfunctional state of much of our world and the past pains suffered by countless innocent people — when I look at these problems and ask, "Who can set this right?" — Jesus alone stands out to me as the place I see God working to make everything new.

Pascal called Jesus "The key that fits the human lock,"[65] and it's like that for me. I read countless books about the history and theories behind the stories told of Jesus—reasons to believe and reasons to doubt. I am as aware as most of the places in the last two thousand years that those who have claimed to be Christians failed in spectacular and ruthless fashion. For every ten complaints about the way Christians act from those outside the church, I can add ten more. The Bible is filled with stories I have difficulty understanding if God is both surpassingly good and powerful. I am quite aware in my own life of the times God seems hidden. Sometimes I have answers to such problems. Sometimes I don't. But when considering God, these problems are not the most pressing detail on my radar.

Death and evil and meaninglessness are.

If God does not act, my life is hopeless, and in Jesus' actions alone—in the whole spectrum of religious speculations, theories, and icons—I find reason for hope. I simply see no other theory that adequately confronts the most significant problem at hand.[66]

In Jesus, I see a man touching those who, because of sickness, had not been touched in years. I see a man speaking to those who had not been spoken to with kindness all their lives. I see a man pushing back evil and leading the world toward a new future. I had thought that if God was real he would look more like Zeus coming on the clouds with thunder in his voice and lightening in his hands, but then I see this man.

Jesus has repainted the image of deity for me.

I am compelled to consider that here, in this man, heaven and earth overlap. Here, the God I have been looking for has begun to make himself known. Yet it is how Jesus speaks about the elimination of evil, how he gives evidence of that future, and how he addresses evil in his own actions and death that I find more compelling still. We will take up these topics in the next three chapters.

NOTES

30   A few historic notes here. The best guess on Jesus birthday is 4 BC (That's right, Jesus was probably born 4 years before Christ) and his public ministry began somewhere around the year 30. He most likely died in 33 CE, and this places his most likely age at death near 37, not 33 as is often suggested. Second, there are good reasons to think that Jesus was poor and that his father had died somewhere between Jesus' 13th and 34th birthday. First, his family lived first in Nazareth and later Capernaum; as such they did not live in Bethlehem where Joseph's ancestors had once owned property. Not owning property explains why Jesus' father worked as a carpenter. Joseph did not work as a "farmer" on his own land. Instead he built goods for other people where he could find work. Because land was the primary asset of the day and so highly valued in Jewish culture, Joseph's profession coupled with the family's mobility makes it clear that Jesus' family was poor. Lastly, Joseph had certainly died by the time Jesus began his public career. Joseph's wife Mary is consistently pictured alone in the Gospels, and in John's story one of Jesus' students is charged with her care after Jesus' own death.

31   This would include his cousin John, who was Jesus' same age and regarded by many in his country as a holy man. Jesus took many of the themes and emphases in John's work up: return from exile, God as king, and the counter-temple movement. As such, we may certainly include John the Baptist as a teacher of Jesus, and perhaps go so far as to call Jesus one of John's disciples.

32   This pattern is one of the few early details we have of Jesus' life (Luke 2:41-51), and this particular temple visit related in Luke was very likely passed on as an actual memory of his mother's (Luke 2:51).

33   Because saying the revolution-soaked things Jesus did in the population centers would have lead to his death far more quickly.

34   I think John placed Jesus actions in the temple early in his Gospel, not because John was interested in chronology, but because he chiastically wanted to pair the temple actions at the beginning with the trial and crucifixion at the end.

35   In the realm of historical Jesus research, both secular and religious, there's little doubt that Jesus did things that his contemporaries saw as miraculous. We may consider, for example, the conclusion of Rudolf Bultmann, a skeptical historian of the last century, "The Christian fellowship was convinced that Jesus had done miracles and they told many stories of miracles about him. Most of these stories contained in the gospels are legendary or are at least dressed up with legend. But, there can be no doubt that Jesus did such deeds, which were, in his and his contemporaries' understanding, miracles; that is to say, events that were the result of supernatural divine causality" (Rudolf Bultmann, *Jesus*. (Berlin, 1926), p. 159).

36   For example, John 5:19-21

37   See Genesis 1:5, 8, 13, 19, 23, 31.

38   Ex. Matthew 8:14-15, 9:2-7, 12:10-13.

39   Ex. Mark 7:31-37, 8:22-26.

40   Mark 1:40-42, 5:25-29.

41   Matthew 22:50-51

42   Ex. Mark 5:1-15

43   Mark 6:35-44, 4:37-41, 5:22-24, 38-42, Luke 7:11-15, John 11:1-44. Of all that we experience, death is the least natural aspect of our experiences. When we speak of the problem of evil, it is established and propelled by death; Jesus demonstrated that he was the God who was not silent in the face of such evil, but was actively working to destroy death and purge it from his world. He has no rivals here.

44   Matthew 19:28

45   Also used in Titus 3:5 to describe the rebirth of a human person.

46   Matthew 12:32, Mark 10:30, Luke 18:30, 20:35. Paired frequently with "the end of the age" (Matthew 13:39,40,49, 24:3, 28:20) and contrasted with "the present age" or "this age" Mark 10:30, Luke 18:30, 20:34.

47   Mark 1:15, my translation of *engizo*. A variety of modern translations translate this passage as: the kingdom of God "is at hand," "has come near," "is approaching," "is almost here," "is gathering around." See Scot McKnight. *A New Vision for Israel*. Grand Rapids: Eerdmans, 1999. 71-84.

48   Note, for example, how Jesus speaks of the Kingdom of Heaven in Matthew 13.

49   This is not only true with the phrase "the kingdom of heaven" which is clearly about God's kingly rule (ex Matthew 4:17, 13:31, 33, 44, 18:4, 23:13). Consider also Luke 15:18,21 in which heaven is synonymous with God's presence and reality. Heaven is used in a variety of other ways in the New Testament, and can also refer to the sky (ex Matthew 8:20) and the "heavenly bodies" (ex Ephesians 4:10, Hebrews 7:26), and Jesus frequently depicted heaven as the location God dwells (Matthew 5:16, 12:50).

50   Luke 15:24, and repeated in 15:32.

51   Mark 6:56

52   Throughout Matthew's gospel, Jesus predicts the fall of the temple in Jerusalem which occurred in 70 CE.

53   Note, for example, the image of rising in the parables of the Prodigal Son, the Good Samaritan, the Mustard Seed, the Workers in the Vineyard, the Rich man and Lazarus.

54   Mark 4:4-8

55   Genesis 1:28

56   Consider Matthew 3:8-10, 7:16-20, and 12:33 for more on this image.

57   John 14:6

58   Mark 14:58, John 2:19

59   Daniel 7:13-14

60   Mark 4:35. The reference to darkness coming here is important to Mark's telling of the story.

61   Mark 4:35-39

62   Genesis 1:1-2.

63   A similar story occurs two chapters later in Mark (6:47-51), when Jesus walks out on to the sea in the middle of another gale. As he again hovered over the waters, his disciples thought he was a ghost—dare we say "spirit" (Genesis 1:2). The images the writer paints all emphasize the point he wishes to bring home about Jesus. Not only is Jesus God, but he is bringing forth a new creation, a second Genesis.

64   "Joseph saw where he was laid" (Mark 15:47) and "see the place where he laid him." (Mark 16:6)

65   Quoted in Peter Kreeft. *Christianity for Modern Pagans*. Fort Collins: Ignatius, 1993. 279.

66   Obviously that would take a significant amount of time and work to prove. I will leave it to the reader to offer a second option.

He stumbled into faith and thought, "God this is all there is."
The pictures in his mind arose, and began to breathe.

Regina Spektor
Blue Lips

4 ENGAGED

When I was young, I threw a rock through the window of an old car in my alley. The glass broke easily and the hole remained for a week or so until it was closed with a black trash bag. The owner confronted me about the window (I was the kid next door and the most likely rock-thrower). I didn't own up and I wasn't able to fix the damage. A few months later I escaped the knowing eyes of our neighbor. My family moved across town, and my last memory of my childhood home was driving away and looking at the Buick with the missing window.

Recently a photographer friend of mine did an art show featuring some broken items transformed. The first picture was of a bus with a shattered windshield, and the picture brought me back to that alley and my neighbor's Buick. Looking at the picture, feelings of guilt from my past flared up for me, and then the slide changed.

The new photograph was not of a bus with a brand new windshield like I expected. Instead the shot was of all the broken glass carefully collected, dyed, and reassembled in an elaborate mosaic. The mosaic was beautiful, far more impressive than a replaced windshield. Someone had removed all those shards of glass in turn and envisioned a future for them all.

ESCAPE VS REPAIR

Often when we think of heaven, what comes to mind is escape. According to Medieval art and modern cartoons, "heaven" is about leaving this world. Heaven is about getting as far away from what we and others have broken as possible. Perhaps we think this world is so base, so painful, so irreparably shattered to fix that our only hope is to leave. As such, "salvation" isn't about a new life, a transformed character, or a brilliant new experience of God and his priorities. Salvation is about departure. Salvation is about "going to heaven," being rescued from this dysfunctional world, and entering a new home that is pristine and trash bag-free.

There's nothing wrong with not wanting to suffer any more, or wanting to be with God (which are some of the things that come to my mind when thinking of heaven). But when Jesus taught about heaven, he never spoke of it as a distant land of clouds, bathrobes, and harp music waiting for the souls of the dead (which sounds a bit more like hell to me). Instead, Jesus spoke of "the kingdom of heaven." It was arguably his favorite topic. Jesus referred to this kingdom over one hundred times—more than he spoke of peace, money, and love combined. Apparently "the kingdom" aspect of heaven *was vital* to Jesus.

But notice, kingdoms are power structures. Kingdoms are areas of authority. In fact, Jesus said only once, "The Kingdom of Heaven *will be like...*"[67] He instead put the here and now spin on God's work and said, "the Kingdom of heaven *is like...*" Jesus emphasized—above everything else—heaven's *present* power, heaven's *present* work. When Jesus told stories that began with similes (such as, 'the kingdom of heaven is like a man sowing seed in a barren field'), he was showing his culture what it looked like when heaven was in control, what it looked like when "God's will was done on earth."[68] We might say that *because* "God so loved the world that he gave his only Son" it makes sense that the Son's highest concern would be repairing the world his Father loves.

And this is precisely what Jesus did.

Remember his priorities: Jesus healed the sick, the paralyzed, and those whose hands didn't work as they should. He made the deaf hear, the mute speak, and the blind see. Jesus cured diseases, repaired works of violence, and cast away self-destructive forces. *Each of these miracles is an act of repair.* Jesus did not scrap the old and replace it with something else. God's creation had gone wrong, but Jesus did not leave it covered with a black trash bag. Instead, Jesus began to work, collecting each shattered piece he saw and setting them all in a new, brilliant order.

When one early Christian named Paul spoke of this movement, he used the word *dikaioo*, which is often translated "justified," as though something is being made "just." We have this idea that justice is about a legal process; but the ancient Greeks and Hebrews saw justice as a state of affairs in which everything is put in order and made harmonious. In fact, "*dikaioo*, 'to justify,' can be said to indicate the *creation* of something, the *making* of something."[69] For Paul, God's remaking activity is the center of all God is doing.[70] For God loves to take bent lives and make them straight. He loves to take an out-of-joint bone and set it back in place—back in tune with how things ought to function, back into the flow of wisdom.

NOW AND NOT YET

There was once a group of friends who got lost in a forest. They had always liked the outdoors but they weren't very skilled at wilderness survival. Realizing they were lost, one pulled out his cell phone and called a man of skills to come and save them. The man said he would love to come, but that it might take him a while to get there. In the mean time, the man gave the group a handful of clues on how to survive in the wilderness. The man taught them, not how to battle the elements (as though they were bad), but how to live in tune with the world all around them as they waited for rescue.

As the lost group began putting the teachings into practice, they found more and more that they loved the wilderness, even though it was very difficult having to create their own shelters, gather and grow their own food, suffer through sicknesses, and protect themselves from insects and storms. They experienced real connection.

After many weeks, the man arrived to help the lost group, with a large—perhaps too large—set of supplies. The man got out of his rig and immediately began working on a series of homes perfectly suited to the wilderness in which the lost group could live.

"Haven't you come to save us?" asked the people.

"Of course," the friend said. And with that he continued and brought to completion the work the group had already started. He took the shelters they had begun and finished them. He took their awkward gardens and enhanced them. He completed the spaces they had made to escape the bugs and storms. He brought order to it all, and the group that had once been stuck in a deadly wilderness awaiting rescue suddenly knew they were not lost any longer.

They knew they were home.

How do we understand what our future will look like if we're not trying to go somewhere else when we die? The Bible is actually quite clear on this point. Jesus and the early Christian writings *consistently* speak in a way that suggests that heaven—the sphere of God's reign, presence, and repairing power—is both *already here* in one way and *not yet* fully here in another.

Again, Paul expressed this in many of his well-known metaphors. He wrote, we experience now "the spirit of adoption by whom we cry Father;" *yet* we await "the redemption of our bodies."[71] He wrote, "When you believed, you were marked in him with a seal [now], the promised Holy Spirit, who is a deposit guaranteeing our inheritance until the [restoration then]."[72] He ended one of his greatest writings with these images, "For *now* we see only a reflection as in a mirror; then we shall see face to face. Now I know in part; *then* I shall know fully, even as I am fully known."[73]

Paul built on the *now* and *not yet* thinking Jesus himself used. "A time is coming and has now come," Jesus said, "when the dead will hear the voice of the Son of God and those who hear will live."[74] Heaven is experienced now in part and in the future in full, and it won't be somewhere else, for Jesus expected both now and in the age to come, the resurrection of corpses. All of these passages point to a profound truth. Apparently Jesus was starting something—and it wasn't a new religion. Jesus sought the reconstruction of our world—through his teachings, through his miracles, through his death and resurrection—which we will look at shortly. What is fascinating to me is that God's repair of the world was not a shock to Jesus' audience. In fact they already expected it.

THE AGE TO COME

In the Jewish mind of the first century, history was often split into "the present age" and "the age to come."[75] Consistently Jesus' followers, opponents, even the demons who spoke to him, referred to a "present age" in which evil had its say, but they likewise spoke of "the age to come" in which God would destroy evil and death.

Of course, the present age is something we experience in difficult sometimes brutal ways; it is clear to all that evil and death have real power. But Jesus' culture held out hope that this would not always be so, that a new day was coming in which God would judge evil and eliminate it from his world. We might think of the view this way:

NOW
The reign of sin and death
The Present Age

THEN
The Kingdom of Heaven
The Age to Come

THE RENEWAL OF ALL THINGS[76]

Jesus certainly thought there would be a coming transformation. As we saw earlier, Jesus spoke of the transition from the present age into the age to come as "the renewal of all things."[77] Jesus believed that God would act decisively at the end of the present age to eliminate evil and launch a new creation.

Put all the images Jesus used together: God's will being done on earth as it is in heaven, the resurrection of the dead, parables like those of a sower entering a neglected garden (read: "Eden") and spreading seeds that grew into an all-consuming harvest, blessings on the poor in spirit, the mourning, and the meek who "will inherit the earth", miracles repairing the sick and casting away evil, signs in which God's Son provided both bread, fish and new wine to those in need here. These images, and many more, picture heaven suddenly born in our midst and transforming the earth, right now.

Jesus and his culture expected a resurrection of the dead, present age. Jesus' actions were signs that the coming union of heaven and earth is certain, but the New Testament also argues that Jesus' miraculous life is not the only evidence we have of this coming transformation. The hints of God's future continue all around us. Let me tell a story.

CHASING US

My oldest son has a mild form of Autism that we have been wrestling with for years. He just entered kindergarten and this was a big event for us. My son began speaking very late and, although he excels in sixth grade math, his ability to function socially in a classroom was questionable. Watching his difficulties has been a place of real fear for me, not because I think he won't do well in school, but because I can imagine these difficulties leading my son into a disconnected, lonesome life.

I recently began helping out in my son's kindergarten class on Fridays. My jobs include making sure the kids are drawing inside the lines and keeping them from eating paste. It's a fun gig, and not without benefits (I have 20 new friends who will all share their markers with me). Recently, the class was doing an art project and my son asked me for his scissors. I remembered buying him a pair, so I asked the teacher where his scissors were. "Oh, we took them away yesterday," she said. "He was opening and closing them in his mouth." A thoughtful father would probably be more concerned, but I laughed and said, "I totally used to do that."

The dangerous thing about serving in a kindergarten is nostalgia. Standing in the back of my son's class I started playing with the pencil sharpener. I looked at the charts on the walls. I examined the paints in a small cubby and pulled one out. I was off enjoying my own little world. Then I heard a loud voice from the front of the class say, "Mr. Cook!"

I dropped the paints, realized I was supposed to be helping somewhere else, looked to the front of the room…and saw my son being told that he needed to stay in his chair.

I walked back toward the class thinking how my son and I share the same name. We both put scissors in our mouths; both of us are a little too energetic to stay seated. From the back, I looked at my son wiggling in his desk. He is a smaller guy like I was. He's a daydreamer who's socially awkward like I was. Standing in the back of that kindergarten classroom, it hit me with full force.

The little kid in the second row is me.

I saw the places where we act in exactly the same kind of ways—and for the first time in years I had no fear for my son or his future. I know who I am, where I've been, the things that have been difficult—and they just aren't that terrifying. I have solid friends. I'm as successful as I need to be in life. I have healthy relationships and a woman who loves me deeply. Right then I knew everything would be okay.

My son and I share the same spirit.

When the early Christians expressed their hope in God's future, they pointed to Jesus' resurrection, of course, but there was also something else—something more tangible and informative. They spoke of experiencing God's Spirit within them and within one another.

The Spirit that had once hovered over chaos and helped make the world, the Spirit that they had seen in Jesus—that same Spirit was now in them. It was tangible, and they felt it transforming them inside and making them different—kinder, more self-controlled, more connected, more like Jesus.

The shared his Spirit.

When Jesus taught that "the time has come, the kingdom is arriving," the image is of new creation. Jesus believed that the Spirit's renewal—of both human beings and God's world— had begun. For Jesus, the Spirit's work is how new creation happens.

Notice how Jesus compared the kingdom of heaven to a tiny mustard seed sprouting and eventually growing into an enormous tree filling all the sky.[78] He compared the kingdom of heaven to yeast that slowly worked into a large lump of dough.[79] *Both parables imply that the kingdom of heaven is not instantaneous.* Jesus thought heaven would take time to grow here, and would slowly reclaim all the places that had been neglected. Heaven isn't procrastinating. It's excited, and like a father who sees his lost son in the distance, it is running out to meet us. We might picture the way Jesus saw things this way:

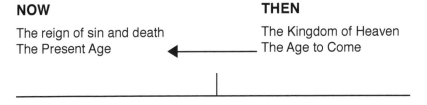

NOW

The reign of sin and death
The Present Age

THEN

The Kingdom of Heaven
The Age to Come

THE RENEWAL OF ALL THINGS

As such the followers of Jesus shouldn't imagine themselves as waiting for the day we all go to heaven. Heaven wants to engulf us here and now. It is chasing us, enlivening us, beginning to grow right here in our midst. It's as though the renewal of all things cannot wait to get started. It is peaking its head in wherever it can. We are invited to become the kinds of people—now—who can enjoy the life God has for us in the future–one of love, self-sacrifice, and gratitude. Even though we may feel lost, we are building the home—our own bodies and souls—in which we will live forever.[80]

RING

Last night some friends of ours stopped by our house—one with a new ring on her left hand. The ring is evidence of their future. The ring represents life change. They are beginning to live now in preparation for their union. The ring on her hand represents desire, a desire for their complete amalgamation. The ring is a gift showcasing the deepest kind of love—a love which gives all of itself away to a beloved.

The word in Modern Greek for such an engagement ring is *arrabon*. Three times the writers of the New Testament use that word, and every time it refers to God's Spirit in us. For example, Paul wrote,

> We know that the one who raised the Lord Jesus from the dead will also raise us with Jesus and present us with you in his presence … It is God who has made us for this very purpose and has given us the Spirit as *arrabon*, guaranteeing what is to come.

Hope isn't believing what we know ain't so. None of the early Christians imply that we are unable to have an experience of the divine or heaven itself. Quite the opposite. The first Christians knew God was real because they saw him transforming their lives from the inside out.[81] As one of them said, we are the ones who "taste the heavenly gift, who have shared in the Holy Spirit, who have tasted the goodness of the word of God, and the powers of the coming age."[82]

The early Christians understood their religious experiences as communicating something fundamental about the world around them. Jesus had rose from the dead and had left them power.

That same power they had seen in his miracles was now at work in them, making them alive in ways they had never before felt. This Spirit then was and is a bridge between the present and the future, between the already and the not yet.[83]

Paul illustrated this idea with the image of creation found in Genesis. He said, "He who began a good work in you will carry it onto completion."[84] Central to how the first followers of Jesus spoke of being rescued from a dead life is the conviction that no one had yet arrived, no one is yet perfect, those who've embraced a life reborn are always in transit. Hope then isn't that someday I will escape. *Hope is that someday I will be transformed.* Like putting an engagement ring on, faith in Jesus means receiving a gift that awakens one to his all-consuming future.

To follow Jesus and to be indwelt by God's Spirit are two sides of the same coin. The Holy Spirit is the token placed in our hearts, the evidence for us to know the reality that is coming in God's future. God's Spirit is the power, the personality, within us; this Spirit is remaking our insides, moving them back in line with the rule of wisdom, making our hearts and minds ready for a future union—the uniting of heaven and earth—the life of the age to come.

The cleanup has already begun; the world is being purged of evil, dysfunction, and pain. This is a time for announcing that reality, for allowing God's future to come upon the confused, the degenerate, the terrified. It is a time for choosing to wed our dead, out of control lives to a transforming, invigorating, eternal reality. It is the time for choices, choosing to become a different person and allowing God's resurrecting power to make us alive in new and unexpected ways.

What other option is there? It seems something must either be eternal on its own or unite with the eternal in order to survive. And this is precisely what Jesus taught.

NOTES

67   Matthew 25:1

68   Matthew 6:10

69   N.T. Wright. *Justification*. Harper One, 2008. 206. Emphasis his.

70   We might read a passage like Romans 3:24 in this light, "We are now *dikaioo*—remade, recreated, refashioned into what we were always meant to be—by God's grace as a gift, through the redemption that is in Jesus Christ."

71   Romans 8.15, 23

72   Ephesians 1:13-14

73   1 Corinthians 13:9-12

74   John 5:25

75   Matthew 13.39, 24.3 28.20; Luke 18.30 among others

76   I borrow this insight and illustration from James Dunn. *Jesus and the Spirit*. Grand Rapids: Eerdmans, 1997.

77   Matthew 19:28

78   Matthew 13:31

79   Matthew 13:33

80   Consider Romans 6-8, 1 Corinthians 15, Philippians 3:21, 1 Thessalonians 4:1-8,

81   A widespread occurrence that fundamentally affected the early Christian community and separated it from being just another form of Judaism was that as the early Christians proclaimed the message of Jesus' resurrection, the gentiles began having the same experiences of God's Spirit as the Jewish Christians did.

82   Hebrews 6:4-5

83   James Dunn. *Jesus and the Spirit*. Grand Rapids: Eerdmans, 469.

84   Philippians 1:6

I am the rising morning.
I am the raging sea.
All things are revolving me
With no gravity.

I am lost in this unending
Song of mine and mine alone.

Tim Coons
Pride

5   HATCH

I taught a class on the Problem of Evil last year, in which we eventually discussed how each of us contributes to the overall suffering in our world. At one point in the discussion I floated an idea, "If God had created a world without pain, none of us would have been invited, because apparently we are the kind of people who willingly cause pain."

One girl disagreed.

"I've never hurt anyone," she said.

"Ever?"

"No," she said.

I knew this student as a kind, quiet girl, and she might have been believable—if she didn't dress with such style and conscious fashion sense.

"In middle school, did you ever hurt someone's feeling by making fun of their outfit?"

Her eyes actually got big. She didn't say what happened (in fact she didn't speak for the rest of class that year) so I assume it was brutal.

GRACE

At the end of the day, hurting other people is the only thing at which all of us are really skilled. She was not immune, I am not immune, and I bet you are not immune either.

I remember exceedingly hurtful things I have said to and about other people—thoughtless, demeaning things. Despite my best efforts, I consistently say and do things that injure even those I love most. Some people have better opportunities to do real damage, but in our own circles under our own power we all willingly contribute to the overall pain in our world. It seems there are no exceptions. Causing pain to others looks like a fully natural part of our humanity, and perhaps we should blame God for such misdeeds. After all, he is the creator. Isn't he the one who made us this way?

I actually find this is a reasonable response. But notice what our desire for God to have made us differently entails. The places you and I hurt others display our priorities. They display what is in our hearts. If God initially made you as a person who did not hurt others—your desires, your personality, and habits, your priorities and wants would all be very different. And what would we call someone who has different desires, a different personality and priorities and habits than you?

Well, we would call him or her a different person.

If at the start, God created you as someone who did not hurt others, you would no longer be you. You would be somebody else. And that would mean "you" would not exist. The desire for God to have made our world without human failure and wickedness is actually a desire for our own elimination because you and I willingly hurt other people. It's a wish that God would have made another universe without us and everyone that we care for (because, unless we have not been paying attention, we know that our friends and family hurt people too).[85] So why has God made a world with people like you and me in it, people who hurt others?

Maybe God likes you.

Maybe God looks at your life and thinks, if I made a world without her, without him, something significant would be missing.

Sure, God could have made a universe that lacked one more person, but he chose to include that person and here you are. If a creator God exists and he knows what he's doing, you can be assured that you are actually important to that God. Not the ethereal you. Not the "you" who might have been without all your mess-ups. God likes *you*—your story, your journey, your future. God had a countless number of different options when he decided to create our universe, and he chose this one *because* you are in it.[86]

Far from moral evil being evidence of a negligent, ignorant, or wicked God—we might choose to see God's creation of people like you and me as a display of grace.[87] I do not deserve to exist. Adding more hurt, more cowardice, and more folly to this world is something I do regularly. A good creator would have been justified in skipping me, but this creator didn't. Apparently, he has chosen to create me—funk and all. This is meaningful to someone like me who knows that at the outset this world has not gained from my presence as much as it could have with someone else. God could have made another guy in my place who would have loved better, hurt people less, broke fewer car windows, and said far less destructive things.

Of course, I want to become that kind of person, but I was not that kind of person at the outset—and it seems that God desires my transformation as well. *Yet the only way for me to become a person who stops hurting others is for me to want to become that person.* I must choose. It cannot wholly be God waving a wand and making me the kind of guy who is kind, generous, and courageous. That would be just eliminating "me" and replacing me with someone else (and certainly God could have made that guy at the outset). My moral deficiencies must be overcome—at least in part—by my passions, by my will.[88] I have to want to become that kind of person, a "different" person, a more loving, more alive person—and I must want this while remaining me—vice and all; for the only way for "me" to reach that better state in which "I" no longer injure myself and others is through my choices.

I find this a mystery. When I desire for God to end evil completely, I am at the same moment longing for him to remove people like me. It seems the only way for "me" to survive the annihilation of moral evil is for me to choose to become a different kind of person, to unite myself to what is good and lasting and soul making.

And to cut off all the rest.

TALE

Once upon a time, the princess in the land of Nunn was put under a curse by a wicked enemy who slipped past the castle guard. The king was beside himself. He realized that the only way to awaken his daughter was with the magic apple from the tree in the middle of the garden at the western end of the world. However, Clive—the wicked, blue dragon—guarded the magic apple tree. No one had confronted Clive and lived, but if a magic apple was not retrieved soon, the king knew his daughter would be lost forever.[89]

Being a strategic, no risk kinda guy, the king gathered all his military men, outfitting them with ak-47s and Hummers. They each considered the map, necessary supplies, potential enemies—and set out. Arriving at the magic garden, the men saw Clive, shot him dead, and ran over his smoldering body. The crew bulldozed through the garden wall, snatched a magic apple, and returned to their kingdom, making sure to run over the body of the dragon again for fun. They arrived home with the apple, brought it to her chamber, and the princess awakened.

No problems. No growth. No real danger. It's not really a story worth telling. It's a heavily armed trip to Walgreens for a prescription apple.

Good stories require impossible odds, and dangers to overcome. Good stories require witches and ogres, a singing sword and a six-fingered man and hobbits and stuff. Above all, good stories require growth. Good stories not only take the hero from a point where there is something deeply wrong with the world. In a good story, those who would make it right are tested, they battle, and they become something more than they were at the story's beginning.

Here's a better tale. The princess has been poisoned, and the ailing king panics. He assembles his whole kingdom together and says, "Someone must retrieve the apple in the middle of the garden at the western end of the world guarded by the vicious blue dragon Clive. Is anyone brave enough to save my daughter from this evil spell?"

A hush falls.

Even the strongest men in the kingdom know that the blue dragon has decimated whole armies in the past. The silent crowd begins to disperse, but then a small hand rises in the back and a 12-year-old boy walks forward. He says to the king in a quaky voice, "I will go…because…I love her."

The king has no other options; he sends the young boy to retrieve the apple. Along the road to the west, the boy meets an old sorcerer who becomes his friend. They rescue a mouse from the clutches of the Salamander King who points the way forward. The boy and his old friend are then attacked by a clan of lizard men who imprison them in the dungeon lair directly east of Clive's garden, but the boy, being lean enough, slides through the bars of his ancient cell and follows the foul smell to the dragon's lair. Once in sight of Clive, the boy, through wit and cunning, tricks the dragon, retrieves an apple, and journeys home having done what no one else in the kingdom could do. He touches the apple to the princess's lips. She awakens, asks for a cheeseburger, and then kisses her savior—and they live happily ever after.

Opposition. Peril. Passion. The story captures our imagination and we rightly consider it a better story than the first.

Let's consider these two stories and what they tell us about out world. The first story has neither pain nor trials. No one acts courageously. The story is born in bliss, ends in bliss, and doesn't really sink into struggle at all. Let's call this story **WORLD A**.

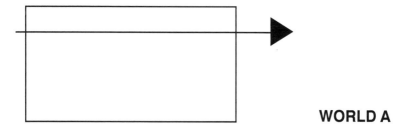

WORLD A

World A begins in perfection, ends in perfection, and never experiences any suffering.[90] In World A, everything is easy, sound, and opposition free—but because of its lack of trials, World A lacks some significant things. World A has no growth of soul. In World A, no one will ever give a sacrificial gift. In World A, hope, success, courage, generosity, and goodness lack depth. In fact, in World A everything we do begins to look like a trip to Walgreens for a prescription apple.

Of course, you and I don't live in World A. Assuming a God made our world, he has instead orchestrated a different story, filled with different burdens and affliction—a story full of adversity and multiple opportunities each day to make soul-transforming decisions. This creator has made a world that seemingly begins in moral infancy and natural disorder. We'll call this **WORLD B**.

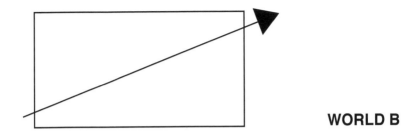

WORLD B

I'm sure God could have created a world without pain or dysfunction. God could have made Eden, or at least an Eden that could not possibly spoil.[91] But he has not. God has chosen this world, and he may have had a very good reason.

When we look at the two pictures—one a world born perfect and always remaining so (World A) and the other a world that begins in chaos but through the free choices of its creatures journeys toward love and hope, joy and connection (World B)—we see that both worlds end at precisely the same place, but World B possesses a multitude of things World A lacks.

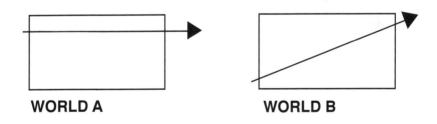

WORLD A   **WORLD B**

World A lacks the journey. World A lacks self-determination, both of soul and the moral life. World A lacks the experiences of overcoming failure, of being forgiven, of defeating addiction and fear and vice.

The experience of World B—a world like ours that has gone

wrong but is resurrected—opens up the realities of love, virtue, and passion into God's creation and into our future. In World B, we can extend grace to those who hurt us and experience forgiveness ourselves. We can move toward a better life and as such those in World B may possess many rich experiences that those in World A cannot. Those in World B can make the choice to become what God wishes for them to be.

Considering the pain in our world, I intuitively think World B superior—despite the fact that for a time World B is filled with pain and death—because World B births and leads toward the best possible life for creatures like us. In fact, because so many of the qualities essential to the good human life are lacking in World A, we might even suggest that a God who would make World A would not be a good God, for such a God would have held back from creatures like us that which was our greatest good—beauty of character, hard-won virtue, and desire at its most raw and hope-filled.

Here's the thing: if there is a God who has made our world, he has not chosen to create a world of the first kind in which there is no story, in which there is no growth, in which stagnation is the norm. Apparently God is not an omnipotent bank president with a big gold watch concerned exclusively with a smooth, obedient show. God seems to like growth, obstacles-overcome, and hard-fought virtue, for our world is replete with opposition, peril, and the need for passion. If God is real, he has chosen to make a world in which human beings are created as moral infants who, through choices and desires, may move into a bigger, more substantive kind of life. If a God exists, it seems that when he considered all the possible worlds he could create, he wanted to make this one most—the one in which human beings transform from lowly creatures into something grand. Yes, with all its failures and its shames; yes, with all its miseries and trials. In a profound sense, this God saw our world as more praise-worthy, more desirable—both for himself and for us.

The logic is easy to see. If good stories require conflict and the transformation of a character's soul—why should we think that a good life would be any different?[92] This God has created a world with lots of opportunities for our souls to mature. Despite the difficulties, the evil in our world may not be a moral failure on God's part. Instead, we might imagine that God has actualized a world in which each human person can experience the richest kind of life—a life of generosity, justice, and passion—a life unavailable to those in World A whose lives are pain-free and morally static.

Even so, World B has a significant downside.

In World B, some will not choose elevation. Some will not journey from the darkness into a bigger kind of life. Some will not die to their infantile selves and opt for resurrection. One writer suggests that human beings are at present like eggs that must hatch or go bad.[93] That's the picture I see.

When I look at the world as God's creation, I see a realm perfectly constructed for the growth of a human soul, filled with opportunities to become a more grace-filled and courageous person. But I also see a realm where the obstacles we encounter can likewise destroy a person completely. If a human being chooses to respond to opposition with violence, envy, and pride, if a person builds their lives on addiction and sloth, if one chooses to be a machine rather than a human being—that soul will have failed to hatch, will have failed to become, and as such will remain like a cold dead seed, stillborn and set firmly in the darkness.

LEASHES

I have a dog named Jack who is currently in the running for dumbest animal on earth. He has eaten carpet staples, a shish kabob (yes, he swallowed the skewer; yes, the x-rays were awesome), and every day he tries to strangle himself. When we go for afternoon walks, I attach a leash to his collar and then he drags me around the neighborhood. Despite my yelling, despite the collar digging into his neck, he just keeps going and going. I've come to believe that he is so excited to get outside and is pulling so hard against the leash that his collar actually restricts blood flow to his brain, leaving him unable to remember to stop.

This pairing of Jack-pulling and Jeff-dragging was our basic routine for a year or so, until I got a new contraption from the pet store. It's a thin muzzle that slides over Jack's nose. Instead of the leash connecting to the collar, now it straps around his snout. The first time we tried it we walked outside, Jack began to pull like he normally does, and he immediately did a flip (which I had never seen a dog do before). All the force he once used to strangle himself, this time pulled his face into the ground—which was equally damaging, but doesn't happen that often anymore.

The nose-collar-leash thing is great. Our walks are enjoyable, I no longer have to replace shoes every month or so, but it has taken all "the dog" out of Jack. The other day we saw a squirrel on a fence. Normally, Jack would yank me across the park as I yelled at him to stop until we got to the spot where he thought he saw a squirrel so he could bark for 10 minutes at nothing. Not this time. This time he knew if he pulled he would be thrust face first into the concrete. So my pitifully amped-up dog just stared from a distance at the squirrel, who looked back at us with his one panicky eye as he chawed on a nut.

Jack couldn't chase the squirrel. He couldn't be a dog. He simply stood there as a statute would, whimpering. The new leash actually makes Jack less dog-like.

There's another leash-like contraption I am familiar with called a belay. A belay device hooks into a rope and allows climbers to freely ascend a cliff side and keeps climbers from cratering into the ground when they fall. You can see lots of videos online of guys crawling up steep cliffs without a belay device, but the odds have caught up to a few.[94] Despite the fame of free soloing, the lack of a climbing rope doesn't make those who slip more of a climber. In many instances they become less of a climber (cause you can't climb well with two broken femurs). Tethering to a belay allows someone to become more of a climber. It allows them to ascend much more difficult terrain, allows them to climb higher than they would otherwise. Tied to a belay, one might become a master of climbing peaks. It seems that some leashes are not restrictions on what and who we are. Some leashes actually make us better.

In the same way, human beings everywhere attach themselves to all kinds of leashes: some make us more human and others less. When I tether myself more to generosity, to courage, to friendship, and to wisdom I become more humane, more alive. On the flipside, when I attach my heart and soul to cowardice, to greed, to fear, to envious longings—I become less of a man. Some attitudes break my soul apart. If those attitudes have their way over years and years they will do significant damage—some of my friends might begin to say things like, "he's become a shell of a man." That is, there was once something great in me, but not anymore. My humanity has wasted away and now I am just a shadow of my former self.[95]

We each know people who are falling apart, who are actually becoming less and less human—through their choices, through their addictions, through their consistent, consuming self-focus—because they have leashed themselves to poisons that will eventually consume all that was once good within them.[96]

I know what this feels like, and I bet you do as well. There are seasons where I drink more than I should, where I wreck the current happiness I ought to experience because I can't forgive an injury, or can't make healthy choices, or can't get my eyes off my wants, my dignity, my ambitions, myself.

The converse is also true.

When I unite to what is lasting, what is solid, what cannot be destroyed because it is part of the fabric of the universe—I become more alive. This is why a common expression of following Jesus is a practice called baptism. In baptism a person moves down under water identifying herself with Jesus in his tomb and then springs out of the water in a symbolic picture of resurrection. Baptism, like a wedding, is a symbol of union. Just like a marriage, it's performed in front of a community to say to all that this person has decided to wed herself to Christ, to the eternal kind of life that holds reality together and is moving it forward. In fact many of the earliest Christian practices—communion, prayer, charity, fasting, meditation, pilgrimage, service—are all acts in which a person intentionally enters an awareness of one's connection with God, the only everlasting being—and united to what is eternal how could we not hope to live on? United to what is decaying how could we not expect to whither and die.[97]

As we explored at the beginning, God's care for someone like you and me is vital. If there is no God to open avenues for us to connect with an eternal kind of life, we will be in desperate trouble. If a God does not create ways for us to experience his kind of life, the problems of death and determinism will consume us. On a basic level, we might call this kind of connection to God "heaven," and the absence of connection "hell."

These are steps that seem obvious to me: death is coming, a God-like being infusing me with new life is my only hope, and—far from heaven and hell being other-worldly, irrelevant topics—heaven and hell are the only realities that actually matter. Tethered to one we will live, tethered to the other we will die. I see no other options. Reflections of this sort strike me as the best and most proper place to begin a conversation about the afterlife.

TWO PRESENT REALITIES

I wrote a book on the seven deadly sins a few years ago. The deadly sins are an ancient list of soul poisons that some early Christians wrote out as worthy of purging. I thought they would be interesting. The deadly sins each have a forbidden edge to them. Yet as I wrote, I realized in every chapter how dull and monochromatic the deadly sins are.[98] I joked with others that you'd think these sins were the interesting part of studying religion, that there was something illicit and mysterious there. Nope. I was consistently reminded that such "sins" are the easy and isolation-prone way we kill ourselves.[99] Envy, gluttony, sloth and the rest can be cute when they are first born, but when they grow in size the deadly sins lead only to pain, enslavement, and waste. In the same way, the hell Jesus described is, in most respects, boring. Often our culture believes an unfortunate idea about heaven and hell that looks like this:

HEAVEN?

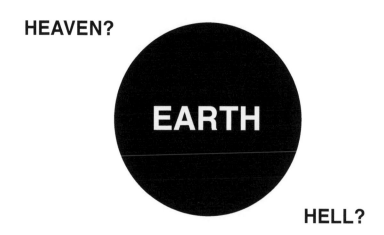

EARTH

HELL?

We know the earth exists. We know we exist. Heaven may be up there and hell down there, but we're really not sure.[100]

This picture fails, for we do experience heaven and hell in real, tangible ways. We see hell eating away addicts who have given themselves to a drug that kills every relationship, every authentic human emotion, every bit of mental and physical health they once had. We see hell destroying all it can through tyrants and the greedy who willingly decimate the poor, their culture, and their surroundings in order to produce a slight uptick in their own personal comfort. We see the rule of hell in bigotry-induced violence, war profiteering, and in the way some human beings cocoon their hearts to the widespread pain in our world. Of course, I experience hell within myself when I intentionally hurt those I love most, when I am self-obsessed, when I give my body over to acts that make my life miserable—when I don't care about anything else or anybody.

We should not be terrified of hell merely as a potential future. Like heaven, hell is a present reality.[101] Hell is anti-creation—the opposite of order and the rule of God. Like its twin expression sin,[102] hell causes that which is to cease to be. It is disorder itself working into our hopes, our appetites, and our societies. Hell is, in Jesus' words, "the darkness outside" where what is fades to[103] nonbeing. Hell is not created, nor could it be.[104] It is eternal only because the possibility of disorder will always exist anytime someone brings about order. In my view, hell is a word describing the state of annihilation more than anything else; it is the sphere lacking God's presence, his sustaining life, his orchestration, his Wisdom.

There are then two realities: one in which the world becomes more alive, more ordered, more connected to the intentions of the creator, more resurrected out of darkness into the fresh life of the future; and another sphere in which what was once structured slips back into chaos, back into the void, dust returning to dust. As such, we should think of our world this way:

HEAVEN

All that is
ordered
and alive.

HELL

All that is
disordered
and dying
or already
dead.

All that exists is tethered to either heaven or hell. Some of the most broken places in our world have set their trajectory toward repair, and some things that appear everlasting are actually wasting away. Where heaven orchestrates the *palingenesia*, the second birth, the early Christians described hell in an opposite fashion as "the second death."[105]

Where many have pointed to hell as a sphere of eternal, conscious torment, it seems to me a better way to understand both the language of the Bible and the rationality of damnation is to see hell first and foremost as "a raging fire that will consume."[106] Once separated from the source and sustainer of life, everything wed to the darkness outside cannot fail to evaporate.

I find it fascinating that hell-as-annihilation parallels what most of my atheist friends and colleagues have always claimed is the destiny of everything and everybody. For everyone knows that death—what Jesus called "hades"[107]—is eating away all we care for. In a world without God, "All the labours of this age, all the devotion, all the inspiration, all the noonday brightness of human genius, are destined to extinction...the whole temple of Man's achievement must inevitably be buried beneath the debris of a universe in ruin."[108] There is nothing more obvious to human beings than their impending death and the disintegration of everything we see.

Again it seems, the Christian and the Atheist come to the same conclusion about the natural destiny of human beings, and the Christian alone affirms a potential alternative: one in which the God who transcends nature, breathes into us, and turns what is destined for dust into life again.

But the atheist must go where nature tells them to go, must conclude what nature tells them to conclude. As such, I find that the best writings on hell are outlined, not by the religious, but by articulate atheists.

In his poem *The Madman*, Friedrich Nietzsche pictures a peasant in the early morning searching for God. The man peers through the darkness with a lantern in hand as those who watch him laugh. The madman stares them down and announces, "Where is God? I will tell you. We have killed him. We are all his murderers." Nietzsche's aim in the poem was not to advance a new atheism. That had already occurred in his culture. The meaning of his poem was to show that the disintegration of God belief had tangible affects. Nietzsche wanted to show that the new expression of atheism was not as freeing as most of his contemporaries assumed, and so the madman asked his audience, "What did we do when we unchained this earth from its sun? ... Where are we moving now? ... Are we not plunging? ... Are we not straying as through an infinite nothing? Do we not feel the breath of empty space? Has it not become colder? Is not night and more night coming all the while?"[109]

This is not a new revelation. Philosophers—both religious and secular—have affirmed for centuries that without a God, the reality in which we live is one in which we have been thrust into an indifferent cosmos, waiting for death to snatch back the life it unthinkingly handed us in the first place. The French philosopher Jean-Paul Sartre goes so far as to say, "The [atheist] existentialist finds it very distressing that God does not exist,"[110] but atheist literature consistently encourages us to swim in that reality, perhaps shaking our fist at the cosmos in rebellion,[111] yet all conclude that in the end the meaning we create for ourselves is temporary and will be revoked.

And Jesus was no different.

ENDING EVIL

Like many atheist existentialists, Jesus described the future of many as a death sentence. Jesus thought God had made a good world for all, had invited all to enjoy it, to affirm it, to celebrate it—but some chose instead to endlessly destroy God's world, to tear down and abuse others, to cut even themselves to pieces, to live in the darkness as though the darkness were real. Such souls unapologetically chose not to *hatch*. Because God favored resurrecting his world out of dysfunction and death, Jesus frequently taught that those who had no desire to wed themselves to the work of restoration and the future God was orchestrating would be united to the only other possible reality. They would be "thrown into the darkness outside"[112] where there would be "weeping and gnashing of teeth."[113]

The picture is of an execution.

In Jesus' language, the image of weeping and gnashing teeth describes two people, a weeper and a teeth-gnasher. The person of sorrow, weeping, despairs at some great loss—perhaps the loss of their wealth, their addictions, or the reality they constructed for themselves. The other figure, the teeth-gnasher, is one who is angry.[114] The image of gnashing teeth is similar to that of a clinched jaw. Gnashing teeth is a frequent picture in the Bible of rage just before it's unleashed.[115]

This one time, decisive, angry elimination of evil makes sense; for God would not be a good God if he was not infuriated with child abuse, with torture, with betrayal, with reckless gluttony that starves others, with indifference, cruelty, revenge, infidelity, with ingrown pride, with the heart that has irreversibly chosen such patterns as its great and abiding love. We all fail. Failures happen in the growth process and are forgivable, *but hearts irreversibly tethered to these destructive behaviors*—who refuse forgiveness and restoration persistently clutching such sins as though a bride—*are not*.[116] There can be no restoration for those who refuse to be remade, who prefer the annihilation of their souls to reality itself.[117]

Some may argue that "weeping and gnashing of teeth" describes just one person, and perhaps this is true. I could certainly see Jesus' description fitting God, who both gnashes his teeth at the infection poisoning his child and weeps at the final remedy he inflicts.[118] But ending a soul that stands resolutely against soul-health—destroying itself and everything around it—is a mercy.

God could allow such dead souls to continue living into eternity like zombies, continuing to war against his world and themselves—and thus allowing evil to continue its domination of some—but *God, being good, does not allow evil to continue its mastery anywhere.* As such, when Jesus describes wickedness,[119] pride,[120] and indifference[121] being "taken outside into the darkness, where there will be weeping and gnashing of teeth," he is describing an execution many of us intuitively desire more than anything else.

This is the end of evil.

It's what many believers pray for. It is what many skeptics accuse God of not doing quickly enough. The elimination of evil in this world is something *we all* deeply desire, even if some human souls will not survive because they will not release their grip on self-destruction. We must hatch or go bad.

The image of weeping and gnashing teeth is Jesus' most common description of "hell," and every atheist I know affirms this view of the human future. These friends do not call their coming annihilation "hell," but they acknowledge—some of them in quite beautiful language—that their own death is simply unavoidable.

It seems *the only real difference* between viewing the world without a God and the perspective of Jesus, is that for Jesus the death of all we see is not the only option.

IN THE BELLY OF THE FISH

My family is renting a house that has a handful of quirks. The folks who own the home are outdoorsmen and it's reflected in the details of their rental. All the handrails are tree branches. They have fireplaces everywhere, and underneath the stairs they installed a sauna. We never thought much of the sauna until a buddy of mine saw it and said, "Saunas are the best thing ever when you're sick."

This week I got the flu, and I sat in the sauna until the heat forced me out. The sauna has a tiny window, dim lighting, and pokes all my claustrophobic buttons. I'll sometimes sit and stare at the foggy window at the top of the door and think of all the bad things that might happen to me. I have this one recurring vision of a face I don't know appearing up in the window, staring down at me as he locks the door and turns the heater on full.

It is truly unfortunate that this is one of the pictures many Christians have of their God. It actually amazes me that some of my kind, generous Christian friends hold tightly and passionately to the idea that Jesus would choose to keep a living soul alive in a place often described as a furnace or a lake of fire. It would be funny—the actual opposite of what we do think of Jesus—if it were not so painfully abusive to the name and image of God. Certainly there has been (and continues to be) reluctance to embracing this belief. Early in his career, C.S. Lewis said, "There is no doctrine which I would more willingly remove from Christianity than this."[122] For me, hell as currently understood is a deal killer.[123]

So too, when I speak with my friends who don't follow Jesus, hell is tops on their list of reason not to be a Christian. Most people who haven't been raised in a Christian environment see the traditional view of hell with critical eyes and call that "hell" what it is: cruel, unnecessary, and out of character for anyone who would be called "God."[124]

I believe this as well, but I do not choose to disbelieve in hell. I choose to believe in a different interpretation of hell.

What I am about to write may not be interesting to you, so do skip ahead if "Bible study" isn't your thing. But for some it is important to make the case that the Bible pictures hell, not as unending conscious torment, but as the death of a human soul.[125]

The words Jesus used to describe what God would do with evil was not "hell", for "hell" is not a word found in Greek, Hebrew, or Aramaic, the three languages of the Bible. "Hell" is a word originating centuries later that comes from the Old Norse name "Hel," for the goddess of the underworld.[126] Many modern English translations substitute the word "hell" for the two words Jesus did use, *Gehenna* and *Hades.*[127] But these two words are not only different from our contemporary concept of "hell;" they are also distinct and different from each other.

Hades (literally "unseen") is a word that comes from Greek mythology describing the home of the dead beneath the earth. Jesus did not believe in such a realm[128] but used the Greek word[129] as a metaphor to describe the Jewish idea of *sheol*, "the grave."

In total, Jesus used the word *hades* four times in the reputable biographies of his life (known as "the Gospels"). One recent English translation renders the word *hades* as "the depths,"[130] "death,"[131] and, in the story of Lazarus and the rich man, hades is left untranslated.[132] In the later parable, hades is clearly a place not of *final* judgment, but of *waiting* for judgment. Jesus' picture of *hades* is not synonymous with our current conception of hell as a place of eternal conscious torment. Rather, it is used in Jesus' story to picture dead souls waiting for the renewal of all things.[133]

In one noteworthy use of *hades*, Jesus said to one of his disciples, "Blessed are you Simon *son of Jonah* ... you are Peter and on this rock I will build my church, and the gates of *Hades* will not overcome it."[134] *Hades* is translated by many here as "death"— and not "hell"—for a good reason.[135] The gates of *hades* refers to fences which held souls in death's grasp, but Jesus—invoking the name of the prophet Jonah[136] —said that even those who are taken under will not be abandoned. In the end, the gates holding his church down in the grave will be decisively overrun, for there will be a resurrection at the renewal of all things.

The other word Jesus used which most English translation render "hell" is *Gehenna*.[137] *Gehenna* was an actual place in Jesus' day—a valley where the Hebrew people had once sacrificed their children to Moloch, a valley that received corpses after Babylon destroyed Jerusalem, a valley where the carcasses of those (seen as) punished by God were burned. As such, when Jesus spoke of *Gehenna*, he was not referring to a prison in the underworld. *Gehenna* was a contemporary example of judgment and destruction.

We see an understanding of *Gehenna* as a place of judgment

and total destruction in the words of both Jesus and his predecessor John the Baptist, who together said that at the end of this age the angels will gather humanity up and those who serve sin will be cast into a fiery furnace like weeds,[138] chaff,[139] fallen limbs,[140] or a fruitless tree.[141] In his most descriptive statement on *Gehenna*, Jesus said to his followers, "Do not be afraid of those who kill the body but cannot kill the soul, rather be afraid of the One who can *destroy both soul and body in Gehenna*."[142] The Greek word here for "destroy"—*apollymi*—is elsewhere translated "execute,"[143] "drown,"[144] "kill,"[145] "starve to death,"[146] "vanished,"[147] "bring to end," [148] and "lose"[149] by the popular New International Version. In this view, hell is an "everlasting punishment,"[150] for the consequence of hell—annihilation—cannot be erased.

As such, Jesus saw *Gehenna* as a place where the soul was eliminated. Not incarcerated or detained indefinitely in a small sauna. In *Gehenna*, a human soul wed to self-destruction is finally destroyed.[151]

A FINAL OBJECTION

Because the traditional view of hell is so difficult to reconcile with their view of Jesus, most Christians I know picture hell primarily as a *self-chosen separation from God*. They will say, "It is not God who sends someone to hell; it is the damned who choose hell for themselves." Such Christians argue that human beings alone can be held culpable for hell. The damned willingly remove themselves from the presence of God in order to dwell alone by their own free will. The logic leads some to then say things like, "The doors of hell are locked on the inside."[152]

There are two assumptions to this interpretation of hell and both of them are faulty.

The first assumption is that God has no say in what happens to a human soul after it dies. This is clearly wrong. Not only is God in control of all things, but Jesus frequently pictured God removing evil from his world intentionally (like weeds from a field, or rotting fish from a net, or goats from a sheep herd).[153] In fact, Jesus taught that God alone would choose—despite the pleas of some who wish to remain[154]—to cast some souls into *Gehenna*.[155]

The second faulty assumption is that human beings are immortal.[156] But as the Christian scriptures say, "God alone is immortal." Other passages in the New Testament picture immortality as a gift given to some, but not all.[158] I know of no compelling argument for the natural immortality of the soul. To the contrary, the early Christians and their Jewish predecessors each say over and over again that separating one's self from the source of life will inevitably lead to "death," now and in the future.[159] The logic is clear. Everything separated from *the source and sustainer of life* must cease to exist.[160] If a man chooses separation from God, he is unplugging himself from the only power that keeps him alive.

Thus, hell is best seen as an ordered soul returning to disorder—the breath of God returning to the breather. The images and phrases Jesus and others used to paint hell—perishing,[161] death,[162] destruction[163]—all imply extinction. We see the annihilation of a human being in the earliest chapters of Genesis. After Adam and his wife chose to leash themselves to self-destruction, God said, "[The man] must not be allowed to reach out his hand and take from the tree of life and eat, and live forever."[164] *Apparently, God thinks it would be very bad for those who choose to separate themselves from his kind of life to go on living eternally.*[165] Thus right at the outset, God removes humanity from the source of immortality and, in his mercy, allows them to die.[166] The man who was made from the formless dust turned back into formless dust, and all that was once "Adam" ceased to be.[167] Entering the grave was, for Adam, the end.

But it need not be the end of all.

AFTER EASTER

Every year in the spring, around Easter, farmland will begin to sprout the growth of a new season. One can tell by this early growth, by the first fruits, what the rest of the harvest will be like. Even though the rest of the field is filled with buds that are cold and seemingly lifeless, the farmer will know by the early, mature growth that one day all the remaining buds will become like that first fruit in size and texture. If the first fruit is frail or infected, so too the rest of the field; if it is large and of high quality, so too the rest of the field. The first fruit is a sign of things to come. Notice how one early Christian writes of Jesus' resurrection.

> "Christ has indeed been raised from the dead, the
> first fruits of those who have fallen asleep."[168]

For this writer, Jesus resurrection was that sign, that first sheaf of grain sprouting from the ground announcing to all a grand event to come. The gates of death will not prevail, for Jesus was like the first strawberries ripening to full size, offered to God in thanks—which told everyone paying attention that all the other cold bodies buried in the earth would one day rise again as he had.[169] Jesus' resurrection set the pattern. It was the ultimate billboard—the sign that every corpse is a seed, buried and awaiting its own resurrection.[170]

As such, the early Christian writings do not often use the term "Christian" to describe themselves. They preferred the phrase "in Christ" as a self-description.[171] "In Christ" implies not merely belief, but also proximity and connection. The early Christians expected both now and in the future that God's power was awakening them, was transforming them into what Jesus became on Easter morning. It's no surprise then that the resurrection of a dead world suddenly engulfed by God's rebuilding power is the dominant theme of the early Christian writings. Notice how Paul, the writer of much of the New Testament, describes the activities of God:

> "[God] made known to us the mystery of his will... to be put into effect when the times reach their fulfillment—to bring unity to *all things* in heaven and on earth."[172]

> And elsewhere, "The creation waits in eager expectation for the children of God to be revealed...the creation itself will be liberated from its bondage to decay.... For from him and through him and to him are *all things*."[173]

> Again, "*All things* have been created by Jesus and for him.... For God was pleased to have all his fullness dwell in [Jesus], and through him to reconcile to himself *all things*, whether things on earth or things in heaven."[174]

Apparently, Paul thought that God cared about "all things." He was not content to let them waste away either through human wickedness or the natural course of entropy. Instead, Paul said God is reconciling the world to himself, liberating the creation from decay, and uniting all things in heaven and on earth. The kingdom of God is arriving.

Paul was not alone in his expectations of what would happen in God's future. Notice how three other early Christian writings from the New Testament describe where the cosmos is headed.

> "In these last days God has spoken to us by his Son, whom he appointed heir of *all things*."[175]

> "The Father loves the Son and has placed *everything* in his hands."[176]

> "Until the time comes for God to restore *everything*, as he promised long ago."[177]

Apparently the world is not merely valuable; these writers described the earth as a gift given to the Son of God by his Father. Such writers did not think the world was something we should try and escape from so that God could torch it like a pile of trash.

Instead they expected a resurrection of God's world.

They gained this perspective from the promises of the Jewish scriptures[178] and from Jesus himself who said, "All things have been committed to me by my father."[179] He called the meek blessed because they would "inherit the earth," not because they would be snatched from it.[180] Jesus called his followers to become "the salt of the earth," because salt is a preservative that keeps something valuable from spoiling so it can be enjoyed later. As such, when Jesus invited his listeners to pray "Our Father … May your kingdom come, may your will be done on earth as it is in heaven," this was not a prayer for temporary relief from pain, persecution, or trial. Jesus believed that God's will being done *on earth* as in heaven was God's chief priority.

For me, a coherent philosophy of heaven and hell comes together here.

Because God is restoring all things by uniting everything in heaven and on earth, there is no room in the cosmos for a soul to suffer eternal conscious torment. Instead, Jesus described the fate of all things united to wickedness as weeds pulled up at harvest time and burned, as homes which would crash when the storms rose, as rotten fish that were thrown into a fire to be rid of their stench.[181] The Christian story is of God finally doing what so many of us long for. He ends evil. He ends death. He ends every sickness, and if one wishes to cling to such brides (despite offers of health, life, and transformation), then God allows such wedding partners to take their lives.

What, then, does it look like for hell to be not merely avoided, but overcome? What does it look like for every broken spot in our world to be put right? How will God defeat evil? How will he rescue his world? How will he squat low and lift all of creation out of this dysfunctional morass? What does it look like when God makes everything new?

Perhaps like all new creations, it looks like a death and a resurrection.

NOTES

85   Someone might object with a story from the scriptures that suggest that God has not created us as infected human beings. He created us flawless, and the decisions of our early ancestors messed it all up. Granted, but unless we are willing to scrap God's foreknowledge or his ability to decisively eliminate evil today, we must find a good reason—an instrumental value—for the evil in our world.

86   I think this is where language in the New Testament that refers to predestination ought to focus.

87   See "Must God Create the Best?" Robert Merrihew Adams. *The Philosophical Review* Vol. 81, No. 3 (Jul., 1972), pp. 317-332. Duke University Press. I am indebted to Adams for showing me much of the line of thought here.

88   This may be why Jesus' ethic as reveled/described in the Sermon on the Mount doesn't target our behavior. Rather, he aims at transforming our desires (Matthew 5:3-20, 7:13-27) and our hearts (Matthew 5:21-7:12).

89   I borrow this illustration from Robert Farrar Capon, The Third Peacock. Found in Peter Kreeft. *Making Sense of Suffering*. Ann Arbor: Servant, 1986. Page 79-81

90   We may further speculate that everyone in this story always act rightly, either because they cannot do otherwise (they lack freedom) or because the pleasure associated with right living is just overwhelming (that is, immorality has no incentive).

91   At this point, some will raise their hand and say, "Wait a second. Our early ancestors ate from a forbidden tree. Death and dysfunction entered our world through human choices, not God's." That may be part of the story, but shouldn't we assume God is really thoughtful. He wouldn't just create things for no good reason. He is intentional. In fact, many believe God knows everything, including future events. This means when God carefully selected this world, he was quite aware that the earliest humans (according to the story) would rebel and he was quite aware of everything that would follow. Apparently, God decided to choose this rebellion-filled world. To deny God's intentional orchestration here is either to deny God's foreknowledge or to suggest God is so lazy that he didn't put any thought into the world he was making.

92   Though it's not really a theodicy, I was glad to see that Donald Miller plays out this line of thought in his recent book, *A Million Miles in a Thousand Years*. Nashville: Thomas Nelson, 2009.

93   C.S. Lewis. *Mere Christianity*. New York: Touchstone, 1996. 171.

94   The single most terrifying video I've seen is of this sort. Google "Dan Osman Speedclimbing." Horrifying!! The dyno at the end always makes me feel like someone has ripped the top of my head off and poured ice in there.

95   C.S. Lewis suggests in the *Screwtape Letters*, "Nothing is very strong: strong enough to steal away a man's best years not in sweet sins but in a dreary flickering of the mind over it knows not what and knows not why, in the gratification of curiosities so feeble that the man is only half aware of them... or in the long dim, labyrinth of reveries that have not even lust or ambition to give them relish." (Letter 12)

96   To pre-empt an argument later, this is one reason why hell cannot be a location of everlasting conscious torment. Disconnected to God, our humanity cannot last. It must atrophy until all that is "me" ceases to exist.

97   See C.S Lewis. "Good Infection." *Mere Christianity*.

98   As I heard Rob Bell say, "There is nothing *original* about sin."

99   How much more intriguing and robust are the words of Jesus and his picture of dead lives repaired!

100   I borrow this illustration from Peter Kreeft. *Christianity for Modern Pagans: Pascal's Pensees Edited, Outlined, and Explained.* San Francisco: Ignatius, 1993. 142. (Which, by the way, is the very first book I would rebuy if my house ever burned down).

101   I would like to acknowledge a worth whiled argument against this line of thinking. In Dr. Preston Sprinkle and Francis Chan's book *Erasing Hell* (Colorado Springs: Cook, 2011), the authors argue in Chapters 2-3 (which are both outstanding) that though heaven is spoken of in present language, the same does not hold true for hell. The authors note that hell is consistently referenced as a place of judgment. I accept this argument in terms of the first century use of the term. I hope here to play out what I see as the practical ontology of hell given the first century conversation. That is, hell has in CS Lewis's words the power to work backwards. Lewis wrote, "At the end of things, the Blessed will say, "We have never lived anywhere except in Heaven." And the lost will say, "We were always in Hell." And both will speak truly" *(The Great Divorce.* San Francisco: HarperSanFrancisco, 2001, p. 69.). I think this is a worthy understanding of hell's infectious methods. For more see the Introduction to another of my books, *Seven: The Deadly Sins and the Beatitudes* (Grand Rapids: Zondervan, 2008).

102   And its personification "Satan"

103   Matthew 8:12, 22:13, 25:30. I borrow this phrasing from C.S. Lewis. *The Problem of Pain.* New York: Touchstone, 1996. 113.

104   Some may put forward Matthew 25, and hell being created for the devil. Again, look at my work on the ontology of hell in my other book *Seven: The Deadly Sins and the Beatitudes* (Grand Rapids: Zondervan, 2008). It seems to me that hell is *both* the state of nothingness *and* the location of judgment where one enters the nothingness. The later is made (Matthew 25); the former is not.

105   Revelation 2:11, 20:6, 14, 21:8.

106   Hebrews 10:27

107   As we will see later, this is the Greek word for the Hebrew "Sheol." It is used by Jesus to describe death.

108   Bertrand Russell. "A Free Man's Worship," 1903.

109   *The Gay Science*. Thought 125. Quoted in *The Portable Nietzsche*. Edited and Translated by Walter Kaufmann. New York: Penguin, 1976. 95.

110   "Existentialism is a Humanism," 1945.

111   Some like Camus, implore their listeners to imagine themselves happy. Others like Sartre see our eventual future as nauseating. Whether this reality is embraced or despised, it remains dark nonetheless.

112   Matthew 8:12, 22:13, 25:30,

113   Matthew 8:12, 13:42, 13:50, 22:13, 24:51, 25:30, Luke 13:28.

114   This brief, surgical anger is consistently displayed in the Old Testament with the phrase: God's anger lasts a moment but his love endures forever. Ex. Psalm 30:5, 2 Chr. 5:13; 7:3, 6; 20:21; Ps. 100:5; 103:9; 106:1; 107:1; Ps 118;1-4, 29; 136:10-26. God's anger and love are not equally eternal (which has significant consequences to our view of hell).

115   Notice how gnashing teeth are consistently used to describe the aggressor in the scripture: Job 16:9, Psalms 35:16, 37:12, Lamentations 2:16, Mark 9:17, and Acts 7:54 (in which Luke knowingly and purposefully references Jesus' own use of the picture of gnashing teeth). Gnashing teeth is nearly always used in the Bible as an event that precedes an act of violence. As such, one scholar writes, "The common assumption that 'weeping and gnashing teeth' describes the everlasting agony of souls in conscious torment is the interpretation of a later age, and it lacks any clear biblical support" (Edward Fudge. *The Fire that Consumes*. Lincoln: Verdict, 1982. 172). The closest refutations of this interpretation are Matthew 24:50-51 and Mark 9:17-18. The Matthew passage says, "The master of that servant will come on a day when he does not expect him and at an hour he is not aware of. He will cut him to pieces and as-sign him a place with the hypocrites, where there will be weeping and gnashing of teeth." It may be, as in Matthew 10:28, that this describes the destruction of the body (cut to pieces), which is followed by the destruction of the soul (in the place of weeping and gnashing teeth). The other is Mark 9:17-18, which depicts a man coming to Jesus for help, "Teacher, I brought you my son, who is possessed by a spirit that has robbed him of speech. Whenever it seizes him, it throws him to the ground. He foams at the mouth, *gnashes his teeth* and becomes rigid." It could be the boy who is gnashing his teeth (the victim) but it is more likely the demon who has "seized him" (the aggressor who is trying to kill) who is gnashing its teeth through the possessed boy. The later interpretation is better and would of course be another instance of gnashing teeth preceding a killing ("he becomes rigid").

116   As Jesus said, "No one can serve two masters. They will come to de-spise one and hate the other." (Matthew 6:24)

117   Many of us have seen pictures of the holocaust and experienced those who hoard wealth for no good reason while thousands of children worldwide die for lack. We know the self-destructive cycle of hearts that are malicious, that gouge our world, that focus every minute on themselves—their success, their pleasure, their tiniest, irrelevant need. Such attitudes are cancers that must be removed and incinerated, or they will kill those infected. As such, when a human soul *insistently unites itself* to such creation-destroying powers within them—when that is their consistent, unapologetic mate—that soul aims everything it is at self-destruction, at the void where everything, disconnected to wisdom, disintegrates.

118   Thanks to the immanent theologian T.J. Wilson for that insight. See also the end of the movie *Old Yeller*.

119   Matthew 13:36-43, 47-50

120   Matthew 8:10-12

121   Matthew 24: 45-51, 25:24-30

122   C.S. Lewis. *The Problem of Pain*. (New York: Touchstone, 1996.) 105. I would argue that by the end of his career Lewis had taken further steps away from the traditional view of hell. It would be a mistake to think that the *Problem of Pain* and *The Great Divorce* must present similar ontologies of hell. There seems to be significant differences.

123   Consider a series of blog posts I did in the summer of 2011, here: http://everythingnew.org/articles/

124   In order to qualify as "God", it seems to me one must be good, powerful and intelligent to the maximum degree. A being who knowingly create conditions in which a human soul would

125   Though this argument is by no means extensive or even complete. These are tips of a much larger case that can be made for annhilationism; see, for example, the excellent work of Edward Fudge. *The Fire That Consumes*. 1982.

126   *Webster's New World Dictionary: Third College Edition*. (New York: Prentice, 1986) 627. Also Alice K. Turner in her *History of Hell* says, "[Around the year 1000 CE] Christian missionary monks sent north and west [into Europe] often managed to subsume rather than combat the beliefs they encountered. Thus Hel was originally the name of the Scandinavian death goddess, and the word came to refer also to her realm, just as Hades meant both the god and place in Greece. Hellia was Hel's name in Germania. In the north, the word replaced the Latin Infernus (still used in variations in all romance-language countries), which had in its turn replaced the Greek Hades." The *History of Hell*. (Orlando: Harcourt Brace, 1993), 105-106.

127   Upcoming translations would be wise to follow N.T. Wright's lead in this area. Rather than using the word "hell," Wright simply leaves *Gehenna* and *Hades* untranslated.

128   Jesus, along with his Jewish culture, did not have a three-tier cosmology. Likewise, most modern Christians do not think that there is actually a place under the ground where the dead live in subterranean caves of fire. *Hell it seems must be somewhere else.* Where hell has moved is a question that *must* be answered if one persists in believing in a sphere of everlasting torment.

129   Or the gospel writers used this Greek word when translating Jesus' own Aramaic into Greek.

130   I'm referring to the TNIV. Matthew 11:23 and Luke 10:15

131   Matthew 16:18

132   Luke 16:23

133   Furthermore, many New Testament scholars argue that the parable of the rich man and Lazarus was not meant to be a literal description of the underworld, but rather an illustration of pride and greed and their ability to ostracize someone's soul.

134   Matthew 16:17-18. Notice too the overlapping of heaven and earth in the next passage: "Whatever you bind on earth will be bound in heaven, and whatever you loose on earth will be loosed in heaven" (16:19). As we saw earlier in Chapter 6, it's as though here in the church, heaven and earth come together. On another note, "In some Jewish traditions, the Temple in Jerusalem was the place … where the gates of the underworld were found" (Tom Wright. *Matthew for Everyone, Part Two.* Page 8) The idea of a rock here, and the reason Jesus selects the name Peter (gk. Petros, cousin to petra which—all 80's Christian hair metal fans know—means "rock") refers to Mt. Zion and the rock composing the floor in the holy of holies. Its as though, not only is Peter pictured as the place where Jesus will build his new temple, but that this temple is the place where all will be informed of the resurrection, of freedom from death, symbolized here with keys (Matthew 16:19).

135   See for example TNIV, RSV, NCV, CEV, GNT, and NCV. The NAS,

CSB, NKJV, NRS, NIV, LEB and ASG leave it untranslated as "Hades." The Contemporary Jewish Bible and Hebrew Names Version translate "Hades" as "Sheol" here, which further supports this reading.

136   This is the only time Peter is called *Bariona*, "the son of Jonah". But Jesus frequently uses Jonah as a picture to describe his own work: Matthew 12:39-41, 16:4, Luke 11:29-32.

137   Matthew 5:22, 29, 30; 10:28, 18:9, 23:15, 33, Mark 9:43, 45, 47, Luke 12:5. *"Gehenna* is derived from the Hebrew *gai-ben-hinnom*, which means "Valley of the Son of Hinnom." In some rabbinical texts this is shortened to gai-hinnom, which is just a short jump to the Greek *Gehenna"* (Jeff Cook. *Seven: the Beatitudes and The Deadly Sins*. Grand Rapids: Zondervan, 2008. 190).

138   Matthew 13:40 13:24-30, 36-43

139   Matthew 3:12, Luke 3:17

140   John 15:6

141   Matthew 3:10, 7:19, Luke 3:9,

142   Matthew 10:28. Emphasis mine.

143   Matthew 27:20

144   Matthew 8:25, Mark 4:38, Luke 8:24

145   Matthew 12:14, Mark 3:6, 9:22, 11:18, 12:9, Luke 19:47, 20:16

146   Luke 15:17

147   Revelation 18:14

148   Matthew 21:41

149   Matthew 5:29, 30, 10:39, 42, 16:25, Luke 9:24, 25, John 6:39, 12:25 among others.

150   2 Thessalonians 1:9. "Everlasting destruction" refers not to destruction that will last forever—what could that possibly mean? It refers to a destruction whose consequences are irreversible, and hence everlasting. The same logic applies to phrases like "eternal punishment" (Matthew 25:46), which are infinite in their effect. The same logic applies to "eternal redemption" (Hebrews 5:9, 9:12). The eschatological redemption, punishment and destruction are events with eternal ramifications.

151   This is pictured well at the end of Tolkien's *Lord of the Rings*. After Wormtongue cuts the throat of Saruman, a wraith like spirit emerged from the wizard's corpse. "About the body of Saruman a grey mist gathered, and rising slowly to a great height like smoke from a fire, as a pale shrouded figure loomed over the Hill. For a moment it wavered, looked to the West; but out of the West came a cold wind, and it bent away, and with a sigh dissolved into nothing."

152   C.S. Lewis. *The Problem of Pain*. (New York: Touchstone, 1996.) 114.

153   Matthew 13:24-30, 22:2-14, 25:31-46 among others.

154   Matthew 7:21-23, 25:40-46

155   Matthew 24:45-51, 25:14-46

156   Philosophically speaking, human beings are contingent beings—that is a human person does not exist in and of itself but depends for its existence upon something else.

157   Paul. 1 Timothy 6:16.

158   John 3:15–16; 10:28; 17:2; Rom. 2:7; 6:23; 1 Cor. 15:42f; 50, 54; Gal. 6:8; 1 John 5:11

159   Romans 1:32, 6:23; Hebrews 6:1, 9:14; James 1:15; 1 John 3:14; Revelation 20:14-15. "In the Old Testament, for example, the Psalmist says that whereas those who take delight in the Lord shall be "like trees planted by streams of water" (Psalms 1:3), the wicked shall be "like chaff that the wind drives away…the wicked will perish" (Psalms 1:4, 6). They shall be dashed "in pieces like a potter's vessel" (Psalms 2:9), torn into fragments (Psalms 50:22) and "blotted out of the book of the living…" (Psalms 69:28, cf. Deuteronomy 29:20). Similarly, the Lord's plan for "evildoers" is to "cut off the remembrance of them from the earth…evil brings death to the wicked" (Psalms 34:16, 21). The wicked shall be so thoroughly destroyed that they shall not even be remembered (Psalms 9:6; 34:16)." (See Greg Boyd's excellent summary here: http://www.gregboyd.org/essays/god-essays/judgement/the-case-for-annihilationism/)

160   This is why Peter, one of Jesus disciples, describes the future of some as "extinction." 2 Peter 2:6. NRSV, RSV, and ESV.

161   John 3:16, 2 Corinthians 2:15-16,

162   Romans 6:23, Matthew 10:39, James 1:15, 5:19, 1 Timothy 1:10, Hebrews 2:14

163   James 4:12, Matthew 7:13, 10:28, 1 Timothy 6:9, 2 Peter 2:3, 3:7, Philippians 3:18-19, 1 Corinthians 3:17, 1 Thessalonians 5:3

164   Genesis 3:22

165   This story is one of the key texts to a biblical anthropology. To miss this line and not recognize its obvious implications to our view of hell is to do considerable damage to the message of the scriptures.

166   This is why you can count on one hand the number of passages in the Old Testament that imply immortality. It simply wasn't a Jewish belief until after the exile, and even in Jesus' day was under debate (Ex. Matthew 22).

167   Genesis 3:19. The movement of Genesis 2 and 3 is very important here. The natural consequence to sin, as Paul says later in his letter to the Romans, is death—not eternal conscious torment.

168   1 Corinthians 15:20. Paul, who wrote about a third of the New Testament, composed many letters in which he reminded his audience who Jesus is and what it means for their lives now. Nearly every letter Paul wrote has at its center Jesus risen from the dead; and each letter seems to move from a belief in resurrection toward personal issues, communal issues, how we should deal with governments and enemies, what we should hope for, and how we ought to live now.

169   "When Christ appears we shall be made like him." 1 John 3:2

170   Paul says: "Someone will ask, "How are the dead raised? With what kind of body will they come?" … The body that is sown [that is put in the ground] is perishable, it is raised imperishable; it is sown in dishonor, it is raised in glory; it is sown in weakness, it is raised in power; it is sown a natural body, it is raised a spiritual body.… We will all be changed—in a flash, in the twinkling of an eye. For the perishable must clothe itself with the imperishable, and the mortal with immortality." (1 Corinthians 15:35-53)

171   Christian is used twice in the Bible where as "In Christ" is widespread. Romans 6:11, 23, 8:1, 9:1, 12:5, 16:7, 1 Corinthians 1:2, 30, 3:1, 4:15, 15:18, 16:24, et al.

172   Ephesians 1:9-10

173   Romans 8:19-24, 11:36

174   Colossians 1:15-20

175   Hebrews 1:2

176   John 3:35. This is either John the Apostle or John the Baptist speaking. It is unclear.

177   Acts 3:21. This is Jesus' disciple Peter, and Peter here assumes that restoration is a significant promise outlined in the Jewish scriptures—one referred to in his most important address on Pentecost following the gift of the Holy Spirit.

178   See again Acts 3:21.

179   Luke 10:22

180   Or more tragic still, the meek inherit an earth which is being destroyed by God. Now, there's a gift worth boasting about.

181   Matthew 13:24-30, 36-43, 7:24-27, 13:47-50.

PART THREE   **AND HE SEPARATED THE**
LIGHT FROM THE DARKNESS

6 KING

A few months ago, a large number of people spent millions of dollars advertising that on a specific date the world would end. When the date passed without fanfare, I heard one commentator say, "Making fun of born again Christians is like hunting dairy cows with a high powered rifle and scope." Apparently he thinks ridiculing such believers is not very challenging, and after a while it's not very fun. But this insult contains a nugget of truth.

In my mind, Christians hold in their hands the most profound sets of insights into the human condition ever composed and yet, despite their numbers and resources, they consistently produce the most lack luster art, literature and political thought available in popular circles. I find the "Christian Living" section of the local bookstore—with a few noteworthy exceptions[182]—a disheartening place where good brains go to die. This set of texts constitutes the best our culture can do when displaying Jesus, his perspective, and the meaning behind the events of his life.

I stepped away from God-belief in grad school, not because I hadn't experienced God's work in my life, hadn't read the scriptures and found them compelling. Nor did I leave because I lacked respect and love for people I knew who were Christians. I walked away because American Christianity gave me no good reason to think it was true, beautiful, or good. In fact, I found the converse. This community, on the whole, continues to produce below average ideas, suggesting below average insights about its extra-ordinary God.

I assume I would have continued walking away from this God,

but my path changed when I began reading the work of historians who focused on the first century. I moved back toward God belief after reading very earthy books about Jesus' life, books about his aims and his agenda. Historically anchored material showcased the divinity of Christ far better than any of the contemporary theology I had consumed. It was the insurgent nature of Jesus' work, paired with the events of his last week that hooked me, that said to me then (and continue to say to me today) that this is the God I have been looking for.

And this is what I read.

CONTROL

In the sixth century BC, the Assyrians developed a new way to kill people. Primitive people the world over punished murderers and other scoundrels by hanging them from a cursed tree, but the Assyrians realized when they crucified someone, they commanded respect.[183] The graphic sight of a crucifixion inflicted fear and horror, which the Assyrians found much more valuable than simply punishing a criminal. Crosses were able to mutilate and dishonor so severely that everyone noticed, everyone was shocked, everyone adapted, everyone was transformed by the power of a crucifixion.

If you lived in the ancient world, it's very likely that you would have seen scores of people crucified. If someone in your town was crucified, you would have heard them die, seen their agony, and watched their bodies decompose on your way to do business. Victims often wore signs around their necks displaying the reason for their death, making it clear to all not only what activities ought to be avoided, but also who was in charge.

On a crucifix, the executed often hung for days until their organs failed and their bodies succumbed to shock.[184] With arms extended, victims were forced to sit on a *sedile*—a small wounded peg—to prolong their breathing and their agony. In order to maximize its gory effect, victims would often be severely beaten before being tied, or even nailed to a cross. After a victim died, the corpse was left to bake under the sun, to decompose, and after a few weeks the mangled body of a man, woman or child would simply rot and fall off the cross. *Because crucifixion was not about killing someone.* Killing a person is easy. Crosses were billboards. Crosses unveil who is king. In the ancient world the cross was a royal symbol of power and of glory. The cross showcased for everyone who ruled the earth.

Because of its power, Alexander the Great adopted the practice and brought crucifixion to the Mediterranean in the 4th century BC. The Phoenicians introduced crucifixion to Rome a hundred years later, and Rome became an empire because it perfected the art of crucifying people. Quintilian, a Roman scholar and adviser to the emperor, described his own philosophy of crucifixion, "Whenever we crucify the guilty, the crowded roads are chosen, where most people can see and be moved by this fear. For penalties relate not so much to retribution as to their exemplary effect."[185]

Crosses were the nuclear weapon of the ancient world. Empires were first created and maintained because of the cross. Such empires have affected many different cultures, but perhaps none so much as the people of Israel, the people who wrote the Bible. The Jewish homeland has been occupied by foreign super powers more frequently than any other piece of terrain on earth. The most consequential of which occurred in the year 586 BC, when armies from Babylon parked outside the gates of Jerusalem and starved the people inside for two years. During the siege, the Babylonians captured the king of Judah—the last descendant of David to reign in Israel. Soldiers killed the king's sons before him, then cut out his eyes and carted him along with the remaining aristocrats to Babylon in chains.[186]

The destruction of Jerusalem by Babylon is paramount in the history of Israel, for the Temple on Mt Zion—the space the early Bible writers described as the dwelling place of God—was destroyed, and for the first time since their exodus out of Egypt, the Jewish people began to believe that God had left them. A young priest named Ezekiel described the glory of God departing from the temple just before the Babylonians finally destroyed the city and led the elite away in chains.

During these days of exile, much of the Old Testament was assembled, edited and written.[187] As such, much of the Jewish scriptures are filled with songs of pain and struggle and judgment. But there are also passages of great optimism. Many of the books of the Old Testament anticipate the day when the Hebrew God would return and set things right.

In the days following the destruction of the temple, one writer named Zachariah envisioned a new day of peace and freedom, of God speaking over Israel in a new way saying,

> Never again will an oppressor overrun my people,
> For now I am keeping watch.
> Rejoice greatly, O daughter of Zion!
> Shout, Daughter of Jerusalem!
> See your king comes to you righteous and

having salvation,
Gentle and riding on a donkey.

I will take away the chariots and warhorses
from Jerusalem,
And the battle bow will be broken.
Your king will proclaim peace to the nations.

His rule will extend from the River to the ends of the earth.
Because of the blood of my covenant with you
All your prisoners will be free.[188]

Zachariah did not live to see this day. Even though the temple was rebuilt in the 6th century BC, no king returned to the throne of Israel. It seemed God had not returned to his home on top of Mt Zion. Syria took over Israel in 520 BC, and Alexander the Great occupied Israel in 333 BC. After Alexander's death, rule of Israel was split, and eventually assumed by the Seleucid Empire.

It's clear from writings of the day that the Jewish people believed that these empires would not have succeeded if God was in his temple, and by the first century AD insurrectionists like John the Baptist were inviting the faithful out of Jerusalem—away from the Temple Mount—to plead for God's return. In fact, John, quoting the ancient scripture, saw himself as,

The voice of one calling in the wilderness,
'Prepare the way for the Lord, make straight paths for him.
Every valley shall be filled in, every mountain and
hill made low.
The crooked roads shall become straight, the rough

ways smooth.
And all people will see God's salvation.'[189]

In the first century, the people who wrote the Bible were not only waiting for Zachariah's king to come and bring peace. They likewise anticipated the return of God, to occupy the temple and present himself in glory on Mount Zion.

A point of hope for the Jewish people had come a few years earlier in 164 BC when a revolutionary named Judas the Maccabee —the son of a priestly family—and his army pushed the pagan armies out of Jerusalem. Judas rode into Jerusalem surrounded by his countrymen waving palm branches as he descended into the city. The crowd followed him up onto Mount Zion, where Judas turned over the pagan statues that filled the home of God.

Today the feast of Hanukkah celebrates this cleansing of the temple. The Maccabean revolt seemed like a time of restoration, a time when God would return. But the revolution did not last. For the next 85 years, Israel was governed by the Hasmoneans, a family of kings that had sold out to foreign empires. The Hasmonean Dynasty began as a kingdom grounded in faith, but their house quickly dissolved into religious oppressors and mercenaries.

The last of the Hasmoneans called himself "Jonathan the King".[190]   During his reign, a civil war broke out in Israel that lasted 6 years and cost 50,000 lives. At the end of the war, the king returned to Jerusalem in triumph with many of his countrymen in chains. The historian Josephus tells us that "as Jonathan was feasting with his concubines, celebrating the victory in the sight of his city, he ordered about eight hundred of his former opponents crucified, and while those crucified were still living he ordered the throats of their children and wives cut before their eyes."[191]

Because crosses were not about killing people. Killing a person is easy. Crosses are billboards. Crosses unveil who is king. We see this most clearly in the methods of the Roman Empire.

ROME

Cicero called Roman crucifixion, "a most cruel and disgusting penalty."[192] He said, "The very word "cross" should be far removed not only from each Roman citizen but from his thoughts, his eyes, and his ears...The very mention of them is repugnant."[193]

In 63 BC, Rome violently swept into Israel, dominating its wealth and people. Rome would control Israel for the next 400 years. Early on the Romans elected a man they called "The king of the Jews" to rule the country, who history knows as Herod the Great. Herod sold out to Rome so severely that he placed a large golden eagle—the symbol of Rome—over the gates leading into the Jewish Temple. Many were deeply offended. In 4 BC, after years of disgrace, a large group of students cut the graven image down during midday prayers. Herod was not amused. Forty of those responsible were burned alive a few days later.[194]

During the Roman occupation, protests followed by violent reprisal were not uncommon. In the first 35 years of the first century AD, thousands of Jews were crucified by Rome in public displays of power,[195] and if we are to understand the events of the Bible it is vital to get into the heads of a common Jewish person at this time. The protests which occurred in 2011 in Egypt and North Africa give us an excellent contemporary example of the mood of Israel in the first century. In these uprisings, we saw people devoted to justice protesting the rule of their corrupt violent leaders—people leaving their jobs and families, people who had lost everything and could only cry out in revolt. Such feelings were pervasive in the first century.

In 6AD, widespread protest broke out against the direct Roman rule imposed after Herod's death. In the 40s, a large mob marched down the Jordan valley to dispute Roman control. There was a third revolt in 54 AD when 4000 people assembled on the Mount of Olives, crying for the walls of Jerusalem to fall like Jericho's. Finally, there was the great uprising of 66 AD in which extremists, militants, and a large number of displaced Jews attacked a Roman garrison and massacred all the soldiers within.

Rome responded.

Titus Vespasian, a military man who would soon become emperor, led 60,000 soldiers into Israel, took control of the land surrounding Jerusalem, and starved those in the city for two years. Once Rome broke through the gates, they utterly destroyed the great temple on Mt Zion—which would never to be rebuilt—and they crucified countless thousands of rebels outside the city. Everyone not crucified was enslaved or carted back to Rome to die in the arena.[196]

We should think of first century Israel as a place of pain and disenfranchisement. It was a tinderbox for insurgencies. And it was in this culture, just a few short years before the destruction of the temple, that a very unique Jewish revolutionary lived, taught, and was crucified.

ADVENT

If you have been around a church in late December you may have heard a story about a star, and a manger, and a pregnant couple who can't find a motel room. One early historian sets up this story with these words:

> In those days Caesar Augustus issued a decree that a census should be taken of the entire Roman world.[197]

The Christmas story begins with a king and an act of power—Caesar displacing thousands of people in order to check the value of his 401k and remind everyone who rules the earth. Of course, the Christmas story pictures something that would have been obvious to any Jew at the turn of the first century. Rome controlled people so specifically that it could force poor, pregnant teenagers to travel dozens of miles in the dead of winter in order to assess how much they would owe Rome in taxes.

Describing the event of the first Christmas, the historian Luke says, "Everyone went to their own hometown to register, so Joseph went up from the town of Nazareth ... to Bethlehem the town of David, because he belonged to the house and line of David."[198]

This early Christian writer intentionally paired the image of Caesar with this image of a child being born in the city of Israel's great king—because the book Luke writes is a revolutionary treatise. It is a work of subversion: subversion of a whole empire, subversion of the violent systems at play in his world, subversion of the categories in which human beings saw themselves. Luke tells us about signs in the heavens, which often accompanied a royal birth, of an angel appearing in the night sky and proclaiming the advent of a new king, of a choir of angelic hosts suddenly singing over shepherds in a field announcing that peace was coming.

Another biographer named Matthew tells a complementary story of Persian rulers coming into Israel carrying royal gifts to Bethlehem, of signs in the heavens that complemented the gift of a new sovereign, and of Herod the Great unleashing his army to find and slaughter every male born in the area for fear his throne might be in jeopardy.

The Christmas story is bigger than pine trees, flying reindeer, and ugly sweater competitions. It is about a new kind of king.

Jesus' mother celebrated the occasion with a song pointing toward this overthrow—not merely of Rome but of oppression, slavery, and evil itself. She sang,

> My soul magnifies the Lord …
> He has performed mighty deeds with his arm;
> he has scattered those who are proud in
> their inmost thoughts.
> He has brought down rulers from their thrones
> but has lifted up the humble.
> He has filled the hungry with good things
> but has sent the rich away empty.
> He has helped his servant Israel,
> remembering to be merciful to Abraham
> And his descendants forever,
> just as he promised our ancestors.[199]

Mary believed that something unique was going to happen through her son. Of course, after seeing many of her countrymen and women executed and abused, having been taxed to the point of desperate poverty, Mary's song simply advanced the question that would have been discussed over every glass of wine, every dinner table, every festival and celebration of the past: how does God want us to respond to Rome? How should we—the chosen people of God—react to a violent, wicked tyrant? And of course there were three answers that emerged.[200]

Many of the wealthy advocated *compromise* with Rome. This was particularly true of the Sadducees who controlled the temple on Mt Zion and those employed as tax collectors in the villages of Israel. By cooperating with Roman occupation, the compromisers were rewarded with wealth and power.

The second option was *violence*. This option, encouraged by both the political party known as the Pharisees and by those who called themselves "Zealots," was a consistent temptation in first century Israel. Both parties taught the people to cleanse themselves, become holy, sharpen their swords, and prepare for a holy war. As such, those who would not become clean in the ways these violent parties taught were often mocked and ostracized. Many—the sick and insane in particular—were simply banished.

Finally, those who wrote the Dead Sea Scrolls, known as the Essences, advocated *escape*. This movement invited the devote to leave the city, to let the violent take the country, to retreat into the wilderness to pray that God would descend in fire to destroy the wicked.

These were the three answer of the day, and of course, these are not answers from a distant time. Watch the methods of power-brokers, turn on cable news, read a recent apocalyptic novel—and you will see in our own day many of the same arguments being advanced when someone asks, how should we respond to evil in our world?

It's in this kind of climate that Jesus started an uprising by speaking about a new kingdom.

INSURGENCY

After the imprisonment of his cousin John the Baptist, Jesus began teaching and acting in politically seditious ways. Jesus had a simple message that he communicated everywhere and that drove all he did. He said,

The time has now come.
The Kingdom of God is arriving.
Return and believe this good news.

"Good News"—*evangelion* in Greek—was a powerful term in the first century. In the Jewish mind, the phrase was short hand for the elimination of evil. In the Greco-Roman world *evangelion* was the announcement that a new ruler had taken control of the known world.

Jesus and the early Christians adopted and used the term frequently to display their aims. Beginning with his works of power, Jesus showed his audience what it looked like when God became king. But Jesus didn't just act. Jesus paired the message of his miracles with stories that displayed divine rule in a way that was neither violent, compromising, or escapist. Jesus instead showed God's rule with category subverting stories.

The kingdom of God is like a farmer who sowed seed in a barren garden, and the seed was so amazing the field exploded with new life.

The kingdom of God is like a man who found a treasure in a field, and in his joy he went and sold everything he had to purchase that field.

The kingdom of God is like a wedding that was snubbed by the fine and distinguished, so the father of the groom sent invitations to all the outcasts and rabble because he wanted the church full for his son's marriage.[201]

These and other parables Jesus told complemented his miracles and announced for all his listeners—the marginalized, the ill, the destitute, those who had seemingly been abandoned by God—that things were no longer the way they used to be. God's reconstructive power was now at work; he was reclaiming the world from the hands, not only of the wicked and violent, but from sickness, dysfunction, and death. Each was a target of Jesus' actions and teachings.

Unfortunately, our culture too often ignores Jesus' focus. Our culture instead domesticates him; it loves to make Jesus anything-but kingly, radical, or intelligent. The Jesus we know is pitched more like an App. Plug in your problem, and the Jesus-App will tell you what to do. Or we hear of Jesus-the-insurance-policy, assuring us of protection and neatly tucked out of sight until the time we may face fire damage. Worse still are the portraits of Jesus as a Mr. Rogers—who's there to sing you a song, punch you on the arm, and make you feel good about yourself, neighbor.

In my experience, Jesus is consistently stripped of his revolutionary agenda by both churchmen and newsmakers alike, but a cursory reading of his biographies reveals nothing less than a charismatic genius traveling to each corner of his country, demanding that the dead world around him crumble and a new one filled with life take its place—and apparently Jesus wanted everyone, everywhere, to join him in this resurrecting work.

One is struck by how socially different and conflicting were the people Jesus recruited—those employed by Rome, those committed to violent revolt, those secure in their wealth, those impoverished, those deeply religious, and those apathetic. Jesus recruited all of them. It seems he was quite happy to invite a collection of dissimilar people to abandon all they loved in order to do something extraordinary with their one and only lives. Such invitations to greatness are few, but a recent example serves to display the spirit of Jesus' call.

About a hundred years ago a man named Earnest Shackleton put forth a challenge to his countrymen to go on what he sold as the last great adventure. He wanted to be the first man to cross the Antarctic continent on foot. A few days after posting the small flier, Shackleton had 5,000 men apply. The flier said:

> Men wanted for hazardous journey. Low wages, bitter
> cold, long hours of complete darkness. Safe return
> doubtful. Honor and recognition in case of success.
> – Earnest Shackleton

This is the kind of call we hear from Jesus. After speaking and healing, Jesus invited men and women to drop everything they were doing and revolt—to go with him on the only journey that mattered. To one would-be follower he said, "Sell your possessions and give to the poor. Then come and follow me."[202]

This kind of invitation from Jesus was not unique.

To one group Jesus said, if your hand or your eye holds you back; cut them off.

At another time a man came up to Jesus and said, "I will follow you, but let me first go back and say good-bye to my family." Ever so sensitive and Mr. Rogers-like, Jesus said, "No one who puts a hand to the plow and looks back is fit for service in the Kingdom of God."

To another, Jesus said, "Follow me."

The young man replied, "First, let me bury my father."

And in the measured, sane way you might expect from your self-help apps, Jesus said, "Let the dead bury their own dead."[203]

Who says such things?

The answer is *not* "a holy man." The answer is someone who is starting a revolution—someone who is supremely interested in gathering a following to overthrow an oppressive power *and doing it right now.*[204]

Apparently, Jesus is cranked up. Apparently, he thinks the lives of his audience are made for something massive. Apparently, he wants kingdom builders (what we might call "disciples") to help him announce and fashion a whole new creation right in the middle of this one—by bringing healing and peace; by going to people in dead places and raising them to life. That is no small task. It is a calling which would require everything from an aspiring follower, and as such Jesus said quite straightforwardly,

> "Any of you who does not give up everything he has cannot be my disciple."[205]

In Jesus' invitations we see someone completely sold out to a singular vision, and there's nothing difficult about understanding his strategy. Jesus saw the kingdom of God as so valuable, so awe-inspiring, that it was worth setting aside every other dream, every other pursuit, and dedicating every hour to see it realized. Jesus embraced this perspective to the end and showed, in the most revolutionary way possible, what it looks like when God becomes king.

CORONATION

The week before he died, Jesus descended into Jerusalem for the annual Passover celebration. On the way, Jesus mounted a donkey and rode into Jerusalem to the waving of palm branches.[206] By entering the city of David in this way, Jesus' pictured himself as the king displayed in Zachariah—the one who would remove chariots and warhorses from Jerusalem. Word of his arrival and its potential implications swept through the city where tens of thousands of people had gathered to celebrate "the Passover" and God's miraculous defeat of a wicked tyrant.

The religious elite and the city of Jerusalem then watched in horror as Jesus walked into their temple (as Judas the Maccabee had done centuries before) and began turning over tables where animals were sold. Jesus paired this protest with words of condemnation, calling the temple nothing more than a hiding place for those who had robbed the Jewish people of their identity and the world of the sight and experience of its God.[207]

Jesus actions were then paired with teachings. Throughout the week Jesus told the crowds derogatory stories which called the ruling class[208] disobedient, wicked shepherds of God's people,[209] men whose work—and whose temple—was like a fruitless tree that deserved to be tossed away.[210]

In his trial later that week, many of his opponents recalled Jesus' saying, "Destroy this temple and I will rebuild it in three days."[211] This was not only a declaration that Jesus thought he was the king of the Jews—for only the king could build God's temple—but more shocking was Jesus' apparent belief that the destruction of the Herod's temple would be a good thing.

Given the unpredictable nature of Jesus' work, his persuasive power, and his antagonistic words, those in power were terrified. If Jesus instigated a war against Rome, then calamity would be certain. Rome would do what Rome always did. They would crucify everyone in the region and destroy the holy city.

So very early that week, the religious elite, defamed, humiliated, and fearful, decided to kill any potential revolution with a murder.

On Thursday night, temple officials were able to find and arrest Jesus in a garden on the east side of Jerusalem, and early Friday morning, when the Passover lambs were prepared for sacrifice, Jesus stood in the dock before Caiaphas the high priest and the assembly of religious leader.[212] Caiaphas asked Jesus if he was the Messiah—the expected king of Israel. Jesus said,

> "I am, and you will see the son of man sitting at the right hand of the mighty one and coming on the clouds of heaven."[213]

The answer, like everything else Jesus said to the compromisers and to the violent, was deeply insulting. The chief priest tore his clothes, interpreting the claim as blasphemous, and the temple authorities then pushed for Jesus' execution.

Unable to kill the man themselves, the religious elite took Jesus to Pontius Pilate, the Roman governor. Pilate was Caesar's official representative in Israel, overseeing Rome's interests and ensuring cash flow from the occupied nation. Pilate commanded a thousand troops, and, though he did not live in Jerusalem, he entered the city during festival times to keep the peace.

The chief priests came to Pilate claiming that Jesus was a revolutionary who stirred up trouble everywhere and declared himself the Christ, the heir of David's throne. Hearing the accusations, Pilate asked Jesus, "Are you the king of the Jews?"[214] The question, which all four gospels record and smacks of historic accuracy,[215] displays Pilate's condescending approach to the whole affair. The high priest sought to elevate Jesus' status to that of a legitimate political threat because this was the only charge that would result in an execution, but Pilate saw Jesus as a weak man who Rome could destroy with ease. In order to emphasize his perspective, Pilate made Jesus a toy with which to mock the temple aristocrats, whom he hated.

Pilate's men beat Jesus severely, and twisted together a crown made from a thorn bush to ridicule the high priest's charges. It's as though Pilate thought, "If this man had any power at all I could not do this. He is no threat to me. He is no threat to Rome, and if they had any sense, they would know he is not a threat to them either."

After preparing the insult, Pilate came out and said to the priests, "Look, I am bringing him out to you." Presenting Jesus, Pilate said to all,

"Behold, the man!"[216]

Yet the insult didn't dissuade the high priest and his entourage. The religious elite pushed even harder for Jesus' crucifixion.[217] Moving to make Jesus someone else's problem, Pilate took an ad hoc vote of those outside his stronghold. When the mob likewise called for an execution, Pilate gave up. In a final act of mockery he said to the priest and the people, "Here is your king,"[218] and ordered the crowned man crucified.

The soldiers marched Jesus through Jerusalem to a hill outside the city. They nailed a board to the top of Jesus' cross displaying his name and his crime. They then nailed Jesus there as well, lifting him high above the land so that all could see his body from the roadway.

Over the following six hours Jesus slowly died with soldiers, a few female followers and a young disciple nearby. His mother was there, and so, in a profound sense, was his Father. But apparently his Father had trouble watching Jesus die, for from his cross Jesus—alone and broken—began saying the words to an ancient song,

My God, my God why have you forsaken me?

Why are you so far from saving me?

I cry out but you do not answer.

Evil men have encircled me.

They have pierced my hands and my feet.

But you have not scorned the afflicted One.

Future generations will be told ... and

They will proclaim ... to a people yet unborn:

That he has done it.[219]

As the day drew to an end, Jesus drank a sip of vinegar wine. He said his final words, and he bowed his head. Bystanders commented to one another about how he died and most left to prepare for the coming day of rest. At dusk, one of Jesus' affluent followers was able to retrieve the corpse, saving Jesus the shame of decomposing before the crowds. When Jesus' body was brought down it seemed that all promise of a new kingdom had died with him.

Yet, in God's grandest irony, Jesus' death was not a defeat. Jesus' death was a royal coronation.

Jesus arrived Palm Sunday on a donkey—the symbol of Israel's king. Jesus spoke of the messiah being enthroned and God putting every enemy under his feet. Jesus told stories of a son sent to reclaim all that had been stolen from his Father. The symbols all built on what Jesus had said before.

Jesus had spoken of a new power engulfing the world. He announced that the kingdom of God was at hand, and he told parables displaying himself as king. Jesus said the kingdom of God was like a treasure hidden in a field, and when a man found it he went and in his joy sold everything he had to purchase that field. *This parable is a self-description.* The man in the story is Jesus himself, the field is God's world, and in that world Jesus found a treasure—and that treasure is you, that treasure is me, and Jesus chose to go and give everything he had in order to purchase that field. As one early Christian concluded, "God so loved this world, that he lifted up his one and only Son, that who ever would see him and believe might not perish, but have the everlasting kind of life."[220]

On Good Friday, God reclaimed his world by enthroning his son.

It began with a military escort taking Jesus out before the people. The crowd shouted for him to take the throne.[221] Soldiers crowned Jesus, knelt before him and sang "hail!"[222] Rome presented Jesus to all saying, "Here is your king."[223] When asked by those in power why he was judging the house of God, Jesus displayed his identity to all, proclaiming, "Destroy this temple and in three days I will rebuild it" – a task only the king could order. His opponents knew the gravity of such claims. They knew a revolution was at hand.

When the high priest asked him, "Are you the messiah. Are you the king of the Jews?" Jesus said, "I am." Which meant, "Not only am I your king, but I am your God—the God who has returned to Mount Zion, the God who has come to set thing right." Those in power saw such claims as a capital offense, and so the temple elite initiated a crucifixion. Nearly all those in Jerusalem turned against the would-be Christ. The aristocrats wanted him crucified. The Pilate wanted him crucified. The people wanted him crucified.

The empire had soldiers march the crowned man through the streets as the city assembled to view the parade, cheering as the robed man ascended the hill to take a seat on his throne, the *sedile* of a cross. Those who lifted him up then placed a large sign over his head proclaiming,

This is Jesus of Nazareth
The King of the Jews

Imposters and murderers had held that title for centuries, but those leaving the Passover—having celebrated the rescue of slaves from a brutal dictator—saw a man worthy of the name.

Hovering over the earth, like the spirit of God over the ancient chaos, this newly crowned king, as his first words, gave a royal proclamation. Looking at his killers, looking at his family, looking at his Father's world in disarray, rebellion and sin—Jesus said, "Forgive them all. They do not know what they're doing."

The words were an announcement of pardon; they're a proclamation of amnesty. From his cross, Jesus spoke as a prevailing monarch who, after a long, brutal war, looks down on his land and commands healing through his own reservoir of grace.[224]

What does it look like when God defeats evil? What does it look like when God repairs his world? What does it look like when the God who has been hidden for so long suddenly reveals his face? Maybe it doesn't look like what we thought it would. Maybe his first and most decisive move was to seize the tool used for centuries to oppress, terrorize, and enslave the world and make it his symbol of freedom.

Looking back on history one truth is certain. In the ancient world, crosses communicated to everyone that the violent, the brutally ambitious, and the merciless reign over the earth. Crosses were not just the way people died. Crosses were instruments of slavery. Crosses announced the rule of death and evil, dysfunction and despair. But this is no longer the case.

Because of this man, the cross is no longer an icon of death but a symbol of everlasting life. The cross is no longer the tool of a dysfunctional world but the sign that this world is being remade. The cross is no longer a picture of oppression, of despair, of duress; the cross no longer screams out that God is absent or that death is the future of all.

Because of Jesus, the cross has a different message.

The cross now announces that all that was once sick can be restored, that evil will not have the last word, that God has not abandoned us like so much trash but that he is near in a fundamentally new way. Above all, the cross will never again be the sign that the wicked rule the world, for the cross displays that only this kind of man is worthy of a title like "king of kings." In him we see a new kind of power, a new kind of future.

In Jesus, I see a new kind of God—one who has taken what was most foul and disgusting in the whole world—the crucified man—and through it has announced to everyone his ability and intension to make everything new.

REAL

I have long believed that without pain love is impossible, because real love requires sacrifice.

The love I have for my boys is manifest in my chronic back pain from lifting them up over and over again. It is shown in my recent hearing loss because I choose to hold them when they get hurt. I see it on hands covered in morning filth, a depleted bank account, and the recent massacre of my DVD collection.[225] Love for my boys is shown in the fact that they can hit me, and yell at me, and even say desperately mean things to me, and I will still pick them up after they have hurt themselves or wrap them in my shirt when their skin is cold. Love isn't a picture on the fridge or pleasant thoughts from time to time. Love must be tangible, for without sacrifice "love" simply does not exist.[226]

The problem with love is that it is a sacrifice of one's self, and self-sacrifice is a kind of death. It can be a beautiful death. Sometimes we gain inspiration when we watch a sacrificial figure give herself away for the sake of those she loves. But apparently such love is not supreme. When someone dies for another, death is the one fulfilled. In fact—the reason self-sacrifice is so beautiful is because death has such power. We know that the martyr gives all of herself away.

In a world without the real and tangible power of death, what we sacrifice is love in its most raw, complete and beautiful form.

Human beings are experiential. We know what is real not through mere platitudes, but through what we touch and see and endure. What we would actually surrender if our world lacked pain is love—love of our friends, love of our spouses, love of our children, love of strangers, but even more so a real display of the love of God, for a world without suffering has no crosses. In a world without death, we could not know the depths to which this God would subject himself to display, in its fullest detail, the love he has for each human person.[227] The cross is a fully committed act of love, for we live in a world in which we know that hanging to death, body nailed to some beams beside a highway would be horrific. And when this God says, "I love you" he doesn't hold anything back.

No other philosophy, no other religious tradition has a story that I find as compelling, that gives form to the things I instinctively value or glorifies so many of the mysteries in which life is found.

This is why I am drawn to the Jesus story. For me, choosing to be a Christian isn't an easy intellectual step. My movement toward Jesus is a step of desire—because I want to see all the mysteries of this life through the prism of Jesus. The cross speaks to me in a way nothing else does, for there I not only see the kind of God who made our world. On the cross I see God's character and his aggressively self-giving choices.

Jesus is not a God who is absent from our pain, who sits high on Mount Olympus watching while the world destroys itself. Jesus is the face of the creator God as he enters the horror of it all with healing in his hands and authority in his voice, who dies at the direction of wicked men in order to display in vibrant hues that evil does not have the last word—for of course Jesus' story does not end with a triumph of evil. Unique in the history of humanity, the early Christians experienced the powerlessness of death following Jesus' crucifixion uniformly describing, in a variety of compelling ways, a resurrection.

Surveying the landscape of potential deities, Jesus stands as the only place I look and know that when goodness and evil collide, goodness is the one who will rise again. Resurrection means the civilizations we build, the sacrifices we make, the friendships we share are not pastimes aboard a ship destined to sink. Jesus' resurrection means there is a different path forward. Love is not a flash of light in an otherwise dark world. Despite all other appearances, resurrection insists that the darkness is actually surrounded by light—and the light is growing.

The movement of God—descending into our chaotic world, dying, rising, and making all that was once decaying freshly alive in and through his own risen body—is what one writer called "the Grand Miracle." It struck me eight years ago, and strikes me again today, as the only possible kind of hope for creatures like ourselves.

And to it we now turn.

NOTES

182   Thankfully this is changing recently, primarily in the work of writers like Tom Wright, Scot McKnight, and John Crossan.

183   This method of execution was later called "crucifixion" by the Romans—from the Latin "crux" meaning "cross," and "figere" meaning "attach" or "fasten."

184   FT Zugibe, "Death by Crucifixion" Canadian Society of Forensic Science 17 (1983): 1-13 (Qtd. *Nature of Atonement* 158)

185   *Declamationes* 274. He advised the emperor Galba before his assignation.

186   Ezekiel 10

187   Armstrong, Karen. "The Bible" New York: Atlantic Monthly, 2007. 7-54.

188   Zechariah 9:8-11

189   Mark 1:2-4

190   That is Alexander Jannaeus. Technically, he wasn't the final ruler. His wife, Alexandra Salome, ruled as queen after him, and then her two sons (Aristobulus and Hyrcanus II) squabbled back and forth (67-63) until Rome took over through Pompey in 63 B.C.

191   Josephus. *Antiquities*, 14:380. See also Paul Johnson. *History of the Jews*. New York: Harper and Row, 1987. 108-109.

192   Cicero (106-43 BC). Verrem 2:5.165

193   Cicero, *Pro Rabirio*,16.

194   Josephus. *Jewish War* 1.648-55; *Antiquities* 17.149-67.

195   Among others events we could cite, the Roman Governor Varus crucified about two thousand in 4 BC. Jospehus *Jewish War* 2.75; *Antiquities* 17.295.

196   See Paul Johnson. *A History of the Jews*. New York: Harper and Row, 1987. 136-139.

197   Luke 2:1 is a bookend. This historic proclamation from Rome launches Luke's two-volume history. Another historic proclamation in Rome concludes Luke's work (Acts 28:30-31).

198   Luke 2:4

199   Luke 1:46-55

200   For an extensive treatment see N.T. Wright *The New Testament and the People of God*. Minneapolis: Fortress, 1992. 167-214.

201   Mark 4:3-8, 14-20, Matthew 13:44, 22:2-14

202   Luke 12:33

203   Luke 9: 57-62. Scot McKnight. *One.Life*.

204   Actually, here's a truth worth of note. When a high priest of Israel was consecrated—according to the book of Numbers—they had to skip all funerals, even the funerals of their parents. Apparently, if you are preparing to be the kind of person who can lead the rest of humanity to God, that task is so important you are asked to skip even the funeral of your father or mother.

205   Luke 14:33

206   Many pilgrims arriving for the Passover surrounded Jesus as he moved toward the city, singing the psalms of festival time.

"In my anguish I cried to the Lord, and he answered by setting me free...

The Lord is with me; he is my helper.

I will look in triumph on my enemies...

Shouts of joy and victory resound in the tents of the righteous....

Open for me the gates of righteousness; I will enter and give thanks to the Lord...

You have become my salvation. The stone the builders rejected has become the capstone;

The Lord has done this and it is marvelous in our eyes....

Blessed is he who comes in the name of the Lord.

From the house of the Lord we will bless you." (Psalm 118)

This psalm—sung on the Mount of Olives as Jesus descended into Jerusalem—begins with the language of conflict and ends with pilgrims making their way to the temple on Mount Zion to worship. It has heavy overtones of war and God triumphing over a tyrant.

207   Mark 11:11–18; 12:1-11 and parallels. The act was a judgment aimed at the temple itself—and judging the temple was something only the Jewish king could do.

208   Matthew 21:28–32.

209   Matthew 21:33–46; Mark 12:1–12; Luke 20:9–19.

210   On Monday, standing on the Mount of Olives Jesus said to his disciples, "If anyone says to this mountain, 'Go, throw yourself into the sea' and does not doubt but believes that what he says will happen, it will be done." The mountain they could see to the west was Mount Zion, and the body of water they could see just a few miles to the east was the Dead Sea. See Mark 11:12-26 and parallels.

211   Mark 14:58, Matthew 26:612, John 2:19

212   Often called the Sanhedrin.

213   Mark 14:62

214   Mark 15:2, Matthew 27:11, 17, Luke 23:3, John 18:33.

215   Especially when one considers the stated charge over Jesus head at his crucifixion.

216   John 19:5

217   Matthew 27:22–23; Mark 15:12–14; Luke 23:20–22; John 19:6–7.

218   John 19:14

219   Psalm 22

220   John 3:16 my translation. Or as N.T. Wright translates it in the Kingdom New Testament: "So that everyone who believes in him should not be lost but should share in the life of God's new age."

221   Matthew 27:15–23; Mark 15:6–14; Luke 23:18–22; John 18:39–19:7, 15.

222   Matthew 27:27–30; Mark 15:16–19; John 19:2–3. We may note that Luke has Herod, "the king of the Jews," enrobing Jesus (Luke 23:11).

223   John 19:5, 14.

224   Even more so, Jesus words are a proclamation of light over all that is empty and void. As in Genesis, they are divine words that instigate a new creation—that push back darkness and unveil the light.

225   Don't ask.

226   In similar ways, I experience my children loving me most when they choose to do something they do not want to do—saying sorry, helping me clean up, hugging me before they go outside—for my sake.

227   Christians believe that through his cross, Jesus died in our place and brought about our forgiveness. Christians believe that through the cross, Jesus heals us, shows us the just consequences of sin, restores our humanity, opens the way for us to follow God, and motivates us to live a new life by revealing God's deep love.

I will hold on hope and I won't let you choke
On the noose around your neck

Mumford & Sons
The Cave

7 DESCENT

A recent movie got Romeo and Juliet exactly right.

In the final scene, with Juliet seemingly dead and lying before the altar, Romeo peers into a cathedral filled with crosses. Walking down the aisle, like a bridegroom, Romeo steps close to his fallen bride. He then drinks the poison that took his love. He drinks it down so that he might be where she is.[228]

The image is of Jesus, who, seeing his dead beloved, dies that he might be where they are. As the creed says and all the early Christians celebrated, "Jesus descended into hades."[229] This God fashions his beloved out of the dust of the earth and though they die, this God does stand to the side unmoved as though the creation of a human soul was simply an experiment gone wrong. This God chooses to join them, in their pain, in their dying, in the grave itself.

This should not be unexpected.

Whenever God moves in the Bible, he is shown descending.

COME DOWN

A lot of Christians, when speaking of where our world is headed, paint images of our world diving further into dysfunction, further into war and disease, and they announce such events as signs of "the end." To remedy such "apocalyptic" events in our world, they say God will appear suddenly in a rapturous event and remove all those faithful to him. Such people will fly off into the air to be with God and dwell with him in a place called "heaven" forever.

This picture has been fictionalized by a long series of best-selling books. It's been referenced in political debates on cable TV, and of course this picture has caused many—both religious and secular—to think that God cares nothing for this world. In a recent sketch on *The Daily Show*, one correspondent speaking of all these Christians wanting to exit our world and go somewhere else said, "Now, that sounds like a win/win for everybody."

Such condescension should be expected. The view that we are made for some other world strikes many as odd. We might ask, "Why is it so important to escape this world? Why would this be the picture so many Christians are painting of God's future? Why would God choose this path? Was our universe a mistake? Has it served a purpose or is it easily scrapped?"

A common answer given by some religious folks suggests that

the Bible begins with God making a good world filled with creatures who share his breath, who move in his presence, and who he would transform into sons and daughters.

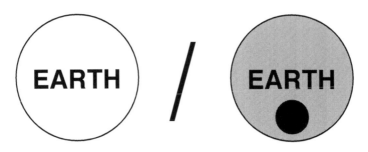

But the good world became infected, not by the will and creative acts of God, but through the daily choices of God's creatures. As opposed to living in the life-giving flow of God's wisdom, humanity tenaciously chooses to live on a different path—the path of stagnation, of the mutilation of one's own soul, of death. It happened in ancient times, and it happens today.

So far, this is a story I affirm, but it's at this point that some say God's great desire is to remove his favorite people from the infected earth to a new location, often called "heaven." The saved are removed and God then unleashes his firepower on all the remaining reprobates.

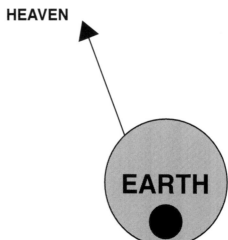

But of course, this spurs a new set of questions. Has God created us here simply to remove us? Did God create this world and then realize, "Oh wait, that didn't work. Let's take everybody I like somewhere else"? That doesn't make much sense to me. God is all-knowing. He must have been quite aware of what would happen if he made a world like ours, with people like us. In fact, as we saw earlier, it is because God knows who we are and the kinds of choice we will make—yet still creates us—that we can be assured of God's deep affection for each person.

So how do we wrestle with the idea of heaven and God's future?

It may be news to many to hear that Jesus and the early Christians do not say a single word about heaven being the eternal home of souls.[230] Instead, they speak about falling asleep, about waiting for the return of Jesus, and about a resurrection.[231] They say over and again that God cares about "all things." In fact, the Bible ends, not with souls being beamed up, but with God descending, raising the dead, and fully illuminating the world with his presence[232] everywhere. It seems clear to me that the primary movement of God in the Bible is not to remove what is good from his world, but like a doctor to identify, extract, and destroy what is evil.

Ironically, the primary passage often cited to picture the so-called "rapture"—the removal of all the good people from this world—is actually one of the first pictures the New Testament writers painted showing the union of heaven and earth. Fifteen years after Jesus death, an early Christian named Paul wrote,

> We believe that Jesus died and rose again, and so we believe that God—in the same way[233]—will bring with Jesus those who have fallen asleep in him....

For the Lord himself *will come down* from heaven, with a loud command, with the voice of the archangel and with the trumpet call of God, and the dead in Christ will rise first. After that, we who are still alive and are left will be caught up together with them in the clouds to meet the Lord in the air. And so we will be with the Lord forever. Therefore encourage one another with these words.[234]

Notice which direction Jesus is headed. He is *descending*. And this is a common movement of God.

In the early days of creation, God descended into the Garden of Eden.[235] During the exodus, God descended in a guiding pillar of cloud and fire.[236] In the desert journey to Canaan, God descended in a miracle called the Shekinah in order to illuminate his temple.[237] During the Jewish exile, God descended into a Babylonian fire to be with three would-be martyrs.[238] In the Gospels, God descended in the incarnation of Jesus.[239] At the origin of the Christian community, God descended like tongues of fire filling the early Christians. And here in Paul's first letter, when picturing the end of the age, God again descends.[240]

"The Lord himself will come down."

More important still, Paul's readers would have been familiar with this image of a king returning to the heights above his city and descending back into his kingdom. In the ancient world, kings and emperors didn't wage war from air-conditioned office buildings. They led their armies into battle, leaving their cities vulnerable both to aggressors outside and the ambitious within. In some instances, those who did not have the king's priorities in mind took control while he was away and worked against the king's intentions. This created a unique state of affairs in which those in power were actually rebels, while those considered rebels were in fact representatives of the kingdom's true king.

We see this pictured in the later Christian allegory of Robin Hood, in which King Richard the Lionheart is away fighting in a foreign land and Richard's brother Prince John exploits the people at home for his own gain. Robin Hood remains faithful, stealing from the tyrant in the name of his king and returning all the peasant's money as he waits for Richard's return.

Now, how would those who have remained faithful to a king while he was away (despite the hardship of living under a brutal imposter) act when they heard him return? What would happen when they saw his face? We get the picture in Paul's letter. He describes the return of Christ beginning with a trumpet sounding outside the city, announcing to all that the true king has returned. Certainly, those who longed for his coming, those who were waiting for the day when everything would be set right again, would not remain still. *They would go out to meet him.* In Paul's picture, both the living and the dead rise, not to go somewhere else, but to usher their king back to reign over his world.

We see this same picture when Jesus entered Jerusalem a week before his crucifixion; many came out of the city on Palm Sunday to celebrate and escort Jesus into the city as a coming king prepared to set everything right.[241] When the true king comes the reaction of the faithful—of those who long for change—is not to leave the city to go somewhere else, but to accompany the one who will end their present darkness back home.

PULLING BACK THE CURTAIN

The return of Jesus painted by Paul is an event often called "the second coming,"[242] but the early Christians and Jesus himself spoke of something even bigger than Christ's return:

> You eagerly wait for our Lord Jesus Christ to be *revealed*.[243]

> It will be just like [the days of Noah] on the day the Son of Man is *revealed*.[244]

> Trials have come so that your faith…may result in praise, glory and honor when Jesus Christ is *revealed*.[245]

The early Christians believed not only that Jesus was the world's true king who would eventually "return"[246] and set all things right. They also believed that, despite some appearances, Jesus was presently reigning,[247] and that he was here with them.[248]

The Greek word for "revealed" here is *apocalypsis*[249] —a word which *does not* imply destruction. "Apocalypse"[250] comes from the Greek word for an "unveiling" or a "revelation" of what has always been true—which is what the last book of the Bible is actually about.

Because God has been here all along, the early Christians portrayed reality far more like the picture on the right than that on the left:

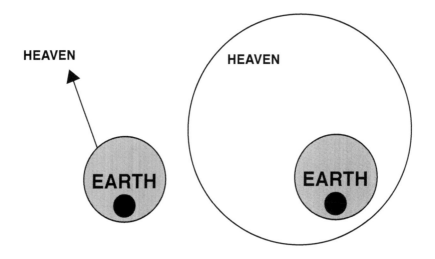

Because, in this reality, the light isn't surrounded by the darkness. The darkness is surrounded by light, and this reality would soon be revealed—*Apokalypsis* –to everyone.[251]

Of course, when this happens, when God discloses his authority and all-consuming presence, all that was once dysfunctional—all the abuses of freedom, all the fractured relationships, all the systemic injustices, all of it! — will be wiped away. Jesus twice paints this event as a cleansing flood sweeping through the earth leaving all that is sound and that desires to conform to divine wisdom standing.[252] It is a picture of a final judgment, a final removal of all that infects God's world. And as such, God's future, "the age to come,"[253] looks far more like this:

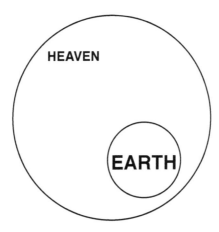

This is the vision of God's future the early Christians painted. It is a picture of the miraculous overwhelming all that is base and decomposing. It is perhaps the only picture available with real teeth and credibility, the only picture I find worthy of my hope.

As I stand back and survey my future, as I reflect on the fact that without something supernatural everything will die, I find Jesus paradigmatically unique. In the pantheon of potential deities, Jesus alone is doing the work of restoration. Many wonderful people are trying to make the world better, but without some kind of supernatural power entropy will erase everything we build, everything we care for—dust returning to dust. Jesus alone seems to overcome such enemies at our gates. He alone has a history of making everything new.

I acknowledge it in his miraculous signs that detail what is ahead. I see it in his deconstruction of those signs, when he describes the world as a garden overrun with thorns and weeds which experiences a sudden harvest—in which both wheat and weeds are cut down, and the farmer brings all the wheat into his home, but the weeds are taken away and destroyed.[254] Jesus' stories and signs point toward the end of evil in a unique and tangible way. In Jesus alone do I get the sense that *repair* may actually become a reality. I see the defeat of evil in the events of Good Friday and Easter, for the cross and resurrection are the sign to all that evil cannot overcome the life in God's Son. I hold out hope that this present age dominated by death is itself passing away and a new day of life is breaking in.

Jesus will "renew," "restore," "reconcile," "unite all things in heaven and on earth."[255] He will "liberate them from their bondage to decay."[256] He will make "all things new"[257] because he is" the heir of all things"[258] His "father has placed everything in his hands,"[259] and he is enacting now the second genesis, the new creation, right in the middle of this one.

And I find my best response is to rebel—to spit in the face of death and sin and the dehumanizing ideals at work in our world. My best response is to steal back the humanity that has been stolen from impoverished human beings I see all around me and, in the name of a different kind of king, to return their humanity with God's blessing and in his authority. In spite of tragedy, my best response is to pause and remind myself there is a different power at work in our world being unveiled right now, in me and in my community committed to this king, and to welcome that power to rule.

TWO WORLDS

Some friends and I just bought an old service station with the goal of turning it into something beautiful.[260] It had been on the market for over a year. The tile was laced with asbestos. The walls were caked in 60 years of garage dirt. An oil pit was in the floor where mechanics once threw used sludge. Right in the middle sat the remains of what looked like a cockfighting pen. An old washing machine and used mattresses sat in the back of the property. Half the windows had been broken by a pelt gun, which was nice because during the summer months the building would hit 130 degrees inside, even with the giant garage doors open.

The week we moved in we got tagged by two local gangs who take wall-to-wall messaging seriously. The city condemned the building a few months after we purchased it for lack of sufficient exits, bathrooms, lighting, and a mop sink. (Who knew a mop sink was so important?) Even after we took care of the necessities, many still saw our building as big, ugly, and unlovable. But my group of friends purchased the building; not because of what it was, but because we knew what it could become.

We ripped down walls, dug trenches for a sewer, dismantled the cockfighting pen, and turned the remaining wood into a stage. After a scorching summer, we added a pair of swamp coolers, and the finishing touches are going into the bathrooms. Despite the fact that we are broke, the building quickly became a concert venue—the only one in a town that houses one of the premiere jazz schools in the country.[261] By year's end, the building will house three local businesses and some day we hope to open the 5,000 square foot roof up for live music, weddings, and Easter morning. We meet in this building on Sunday nights to celebrate Jesus together, but we could do that anywhere. We are transforming this building as a sign to everyone in our town that our God loves to take all that is neglected, dysfunctional, and falling apart and make them new again. Our God loves resurrections.

We believe there are two realities, not just for old buildings, but for every molecule of our cosmos. There is a reality in which chaos is king, in which there is no order, no wisdom, no love—where entropy reigns and eventually all that exists falls apart. And there is another reality, in which what is supernatural descends and embraces the chaotic mess and begins to restore all that was once broken. These are our two potential futures. There is nothing else. There is the one reality governed by God and, outside of that, there is the sphere of disorder. And only one will last.

The picture I have painted through this book comes full circle for me here.

I see unique places of beauty in the nature-only glasses. I under-stand and respect why someone would be an agnostic or a com-mitted atheist. I think that, in their own ways, this perspective is a beautiful religious commitment as it moves to create meaning and value from nothing.

Like any philosophy, seeing the world as only an arrangement of matter initially requires a move of faith. Naturalism is a perspec-tive that is selected and worn like any other set of lenses. Those who view the world and themselves through such glasses live out the consequences and emotional impact of that perspective. Certainly courage, hope, and benevolence can be found in the atheistic faith, but its end is scripted. The story it tells is clear. The laws of nature are unbending and they will eventually shred all that we once loved. Despite such problems, I still find the atheistic picture compelling.

I feel the pull to believe a tale about our world that says; real-ity is just matter, it is just motion, and anything beyond that is blind conjecture. I am compelled by the simplicity of Naturalism. It makes sense of why our world is so violent, so sex obsessed, so egocentric. It makes sense of why the wicked thrive and the innocent suffer without any apparent rhyme or reason. It makes sense of the history of man: our wars, our pursuits, our confu-sions. And it makes sense of why God seems so hidden—God hides because he really isn't there. While I believe in a God that desires to make each person into a child, I think it is a deep mys-tery why many find God elusive.

Mystery however is something I am becoming increasingly com-fortable with, for it is often in the mysterious that I see life at its most raw and integrated.

It is mysterious how the mind and soul interact with the physical brain. It is mysterious why human beings have a unique value over and above other living things. It is mysterious why love is more than chemical events in our skulls. It is mysterious why we exist and what purposes our lives have. *Mystery is where life takes place, and it matters very little what glasses you put on, you'll find the mysteries in the reality you choose to see.* One of the great philosophers of the last century said, "Even when all *possible* scientific questions have been answered, the problems of life remain completely untouched."[262]

In my own journey, I find the story of a world without God does nothing much to address such mysteries. It simply sets the problems of life aside, or hacks them to pieces so severely that all the things I once valued—meaning, personality, love—are left in a bloody pile, reduced to chemical reactions and DNA. Conversely, when I read about the life and, particularly, the death and resurrection of Jesus, I recognize them as central truths around which all the most basic and pressing mysteries revolve and become glorious.

God's hiddenness and evil are real problems for me—until I take that step and say, "I see God in that man hanging on that cross." The problem of why human beings have value is real for me, until I put on those glasses which see God dying and rising for my sake. The problem of the mind connecting with the physical brain is a real problem for me, but when I assume that Wisdom itself wore flesh and bone, the mystery becomes magnificent. The problem of love being more than a chemical reaction is real for me, but when I believe God entered the created order—born in poverty, dying in disgrace, and considering it all worth it—love is no longer one of the anomalies experienced by a unique species in this corner of the cosmos. The choices of Jesus show that love is the central movement of the entire created order, for it is the primary impulse and method of its Creator.

Becoming a Christian has not answered life's mysteries for me. That would be far too easy. Jesus' death and resurrection give shape to them so that the mysteries are no longer terrifying. Now the mysteries are worth plunging into. They are worthy not only of my sustained reflections, but also of giving all of myself: body, mind, and soul.

When I consider it all, I choose to believe because of both the tragedy and the beauty. They lead me not only to a God, but to a very specific God. I understand that I can freely commit to a view in which everything is falling apart or one in which everything is being put back together again.

The choice I see is between a hell and a heaven, and I choose the later.

NOTES

228   *Romeo + Juliet.* 1996. 20th Century Fox. Directed by Baz Luhrmann.

229   From the Apostles' Creed. See also Matthew 12:40, Acts 2:27-31, 1 Peter 3:19-20, 4:6

230   That is, heaven as the permanent home of souls after this life. Some passages speak about going to be with Jesus; but it is clear that being in that state is actually temporary, for the early Christians believed in a resurrection of their physical bodies—here. We will get into the verses shortly.

231   Mark 5:39, Luke 8:52, 20:34-38, John 11:11, 1 Corinthians 1:7, 4:5, 11:30, 15:6, 18-20, Galatians 5:5, Philippians 3:20, 1 Thessalonians 1:10, 4:13-15, 5:10, Titus 2:13, Revelation 22:20—among many others.

232   Revelation 20:11-22:21. Consider one verse here, "I heard a loud voice from the throne saying, 'Look! God's dwelling place is now among the people, and he will dwell with them'" (21:3).

233   Gk. *houtos.* Seemingly left out in the TNIV, but it's vital because Paul is describing what each person will look like in the future. They will rise "in the same way" Jesus did on Easter morning. N.T. Wright translates the passage, "If we believe that Jesus died and rose, that's the way God will also bring, with Jesus, those who fell asleep through him" *Paul for Everyone: Galatians and Thessalonians* (Louisville: Westminster John Knox Press, 2004), 123.

234   1 Thessalonians 4:14-18. Emphasis mine.

235   Genesis 2:7, 3:8

236   Exodus 13:21-22; Numbers 14:14.

237   Exodus 40:34-35

238 Daniel 3:3:24-25

239 John 1:1-18 among others.

240 Acts 2:1-4

241 "Those who went ahead and those who followed shouted, 'Blessed is the coming kingdom!'" Mark 11:9-10

242 In Greek it is *Parousia*. See Matthew 24:3, 27, 30, 37, 39; 1 Thessalonians 4:15, 5:23; 2 Thessalonians 2:1,8; James 5:7-8; 2 Peter 1:16, 3:4, 12.

243 1 Corinthians 1:7

244 Luke 17:27-30

245 1 Peter 1:7

246 Gk. *erchomai*. Another common word describing the end of the age.

247 Which is what the ascension is about. See Daniel 7:13-14 (which was used frequently by Jesus as his favorite self-description), and Luke 22:67-70. These are all about who is truly in charge. The resurrection and ascension are the proof that who is in charge is, in fact, Jesus.

248 Consider, for example, the language of Matthew 28. "I am with you always to the very end of the age."

249 Or *Apokalypto*. See also Romans 2:5; 2 Thessalonians 1:7; 1 Peter 1:5, 7, 13, 4:13, 5:1 (among others). In reference to our participation in the reality of heaven, see Romans 8:18, 19, 1 Peter 1:13, 2 Corinthians 4:10, 11 (the later are again describing heaven as a present reality).

250 *Apo* from the Greek "from, off" and the root *Kalupto*, "to cover" (Vines 531-2).

251   Consider for example 2 Thessalonians 1:7, "God is just: He will pay back trouble to those who trouble you and give relief to you who are troubled, and to us as well. This will happen when the Lord Jesus is revealed from heaven in blazing fire with his powerful angels."

252   Matthew 7:24-27, 24:37-39. If we view the story of the scriptures chiastically, then the Bible begins and ends with God making his home in his creation, but one step in we see two floods, that of Noah and that of the final removal of evil. One step further still we see the pairing of Pentecost and Babel, and one step more we see the faith of Abraham that brings resurrection and creates a nation too numerous to count paired with Jesus resurrection and the birth of the Church.

253   Matthew 12:32, Mark 10:30, Luke 18:30 among other references.

254   Matthew 13:24-29, 36-43

255   "Renew": Matthew 19:28, 2 Corinthians 4:6, Titus 3:5; "Restore": Matthew 17:11, Acts 3:21; "Reconcile": Romans 11:15, 2 Corinthians 5:19, Colossians 1:20; "Unite all things" Ephesians 1:10.

256   Romans 8:21

257   Revelation 21:5

258   Hebrews 1:2

259   John 3:35

260   Yes, we had to leave the Beetle, which is now a Philly Cheese Steak restaurant. We hope the psalm that says, "Surely goodness and mercy will follow me all the days of my life" is true of the Atlas community.

261   In fact, our first gift from a donor was a marquee. Who would have guessed we would think a marquee on our church would be a good idea?

Thankfully none of us are clever enough to create pithy proverbs like "A closed mouth gathers no foot." Instead the marquee just says, "The Atlas Theater" on top with a list of upcoming shows beneath.

262 Ludwig Wittgenstein. *Tractatus Logico-Philsophicus*. 6.52. Emphasis his. Wittgenstein goes on to say, "Of course there are then no questions left, and this itself is the answer."

I want to feel sunlight on my face, see the dust
cloud disappear without a trace.
I want to take shelter from the poison rain.

U2
Where the Streets have No Name

THE FIRST DAY OF THE WEEK

The movement of all life is down into the dark and then up into
the bright sunlight. We see it in every plant and every tree as
each one casts its seeds into the cold earth. We see it in the
union and growth of a sperm and egg, united in the darkness. All
life begins in something like a tomb. Buried and covered, a seed
grows in the darkness because the darkness opens up something significant. Yet the seed is not made for the darkness. Life
reaches up out of the deep, and though it begins in a grave, all
life eventually rises. The darkness is bad only if the seed remains and dies there. Otherwise, the darkness is necessary. It
is the realm of birth.

As in Genesis, darkness is where creation begins.

We began this work with the supremacy of death, and we end

with a God who speaks. Looking on his dead bride, his children, his beloved, God says a single word over his creation—and that word is "resurrection."

WEDDING

Jesus' opening miracle doesn't seem all that spectacular.[263] Compared with raising the dead and walking across the sea, changing water into wine feels like a party trick. Which it is.

The author John began the story of Jesus' first miracle by saying, "On the third day, there was a wedding."[264] Unfortunately, during this wedding the bride and groom ran out of wine. We may assume that the couple stood embarrassed on the side, and their family and friends—unmotivated by alcohol to dance, sing, or reminisce—all began asking each other whether they should head out.

The party was as good as dead, until Jesus' mother came and asked him to do something for this couple. This was their day, the day they celebrated the overlapping and interlocking of their lives, and here, with the wedding on the line, Jesus chose to perform his first sign—an inaugural miracle whose meaning and symbolism were deep. Jesus turned to some servants and asked them to fill a set of stone jars with water. These were not normal jars. The water placed in these jars was used to make people clean so they might encounter God. Jesus took that water, offered it to the one hosting the wedding—the master off the banquet[265] —and turned it to wine.

The party had died, the union could not go forward as planned, but with wine Jesus acted on the third day, and raised the marriage from the dead.

As was so often the case with Jesus, he carefully chose which images displayed his identity—what his life and actions meant. Wine is a common symbol in the early Christian writings of not only Jesus' blood, but also of God's Spirit and the life of the New Creation. Equally significant is the wedding. A wedding is an image of two beautiful, yet distinct realities coming together in total union. When joined, these images say something profound. Jesus turned water (that ancient symbol of chaos) into wine[266] (a common symbol of God's new world) and this work allowed a marriage to go forward.

"On the third day, there was a wedding."

This opening phrase of John's story was carefully chosen and tells us all we need to know about how John saw his world. All of John's early readers knew what had happened on "the third day." It was Easter morning, the day that Jesus rose from the dead. Early in his career, Jesus deconstructed Easter, defined it, and pointed to the significance of his own resurrection.

"On the third day, there was a wedding."

Many faithful to God in Jesus' day were asking why God would leave, why he would abandon this special people to the whims of evil nations. Often this is my own question when I look at evil. I struggle to understand why God would seemingly leave me, or those I love, to fight through suffering on our own. I do not understand why a separation exists between our world and the reign of God. I might go so far sometimes as to say that if a God exists, he has "divorced" himself from the world around me.

But John was hopeful. "On the third day, there was a wedding."

Notice, the wedding in John's story had not yet been fully consummated. The party was thrown, and then it went wrong. There had been a plan for total union, but without the wine the wedding could not go forward. It's the same picture in Genesis. In Genesis, God not only made a good world, but he longed to fill it—to unite himself with his creation. But something went wrong. Humanity rejected God, rejected his garden, rejected union, rejected the marriage of heaven and earth. Instead, the first thing humanity did collectively was to build a huge tower, imagining that they could escape the world God made for them to go somewhere else.[267]

The Bible begins with a divorce and humanity's subsequent refusal of the earth and everything in it—but here in an early story of Jesus we see God at work again.[268] Though humanity once rejected him like just another suitor, God's love does not die. On the third day—the day of resurrection—a wedding recommenced through the work of Jesus, through the wine, through the deep desires of God.[269]

In Jesus, John saw the ancient God entering the creation he loved and offering it a new proposal for a new union.

This central image of a wedding is repeated in John's telling of Jesus' resurrection. At the end of his Gospel, John chose to have just one woman discover the empty tomb and not multiple women as the other Gospels do.[270] John wanted to picture Easter morning for his readers in a clarifying light. In John's story, a lone woman encounters Jesus, and she doesn't recognize him. Instead she thinks he's a gardener; and of course there is a good reason why: John tells us, "At the place Jesus was crucified, there was a garden, and in the garden a new tomb ... They laid Jesus there." To display the significance of Easter morning, John painted a man and a woman standing in a garden. It is the same picture that begins Genesis.[271]

Just as Adam and his bride Eve had stood in Eden together enjoying the new world on the first day of the week (the day after God's Sabbath rest), so too, Jesus' was laid in the tomb on Saturday, and "Early on the first day of the week, while it was still dark, Mary Magdalene went to the tomb and saw that the stone had been removed."[272] The day Jesus rose from the grave was the first day of God's renewed world.[273] Jesus' resurrection moved the wedding—the union of heaven and earth—forward as planned.[274]

Consider an illustration.

REVOLUTION

Near the end of his life, Nicolaus Copernicus[275] started a revolution. For centuries, most of humanity assumed the earth was the center of the universe and that all the bodies in the heavens had been place there to serve it. Copernicus, however, spent most of his life looking at the stars, looking at the planets and their motions, and he, along with some others, argued that the motions above didn't make sense. Some planets zigged when they were supposed to zag. They changed course abruptly or even stopped for no reason. Such zagging and halts were predictable (Ptolemy composed a detailed portrait of celestial movements in the first century), but they didn't make sense.

Instead of viewing ourselves as the center of reality, Copernicus suggested we should look at the sun. The sun was grand enough to be the centerpiece of reality. The sun's centrality could hold everything else in orbit, and this idea changed the way humanity saw itself. The earth was dependent. The rest of creation did not revolve around the earth; something else was bigger. Something else had always been central, and we were just coming to realize it.

I often walk through life as though my priorities, my hopes and dreams, my trajectory, are central. I'm sometimes deceived into thinking everything revolves around me for my benefit. But this is false. Bigger realities hold my life in place.

On my own, I am really not all that important.

Most world religions make this move and affirm something else as transcendent, as holy, as so other that it is worthy of our adoration. This reality—sometimes called God—then becomes the center of a good human life, for we don't really want to be a lonely planet, drifting out into the void of space. We need warmth. We need direction. We need a sun.

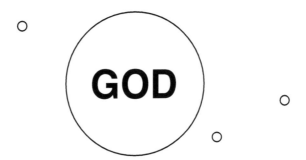

When I affirm such religious claims, I begin to see the world in two ways. First, I see the sacredness of God and everything connected to God—churches, rituals, holy days, and the like. Second, I see my everyday life as something distant from what is holy—still base, still spinning away in its own space. Even when I am in orbit around God as it were, I am still out in the darkness, and so is most of my culture, my friends, and—quite obviously—so are my enemies. In fact, those who disagree with me are the ones who seem to not even acknowledge the divine, and are spinning off into the distance, running into me or warring against my priorities.

This kind of conception of God is common in religion. *However, many of the early Christians spent considerable time and effort encouraging others to jump into a very different way of conceiving God.* Unlike planets revolving around a stabilizing sun, the Christian picture was not one of us remaining in our own dark void of space, hoping that we remain chained to our sun, divorcing reality into camps that are either "holy" or "secular," "worldly" or "sacred."

For the early Christians, Jesus is not only the best image of what the creator God is like, Jesus is in a unique sense God with us,[276] pursuing us, unifying his sphere of heaven with ours. We see the marriage of heaven and earth in his healings as he restored broken bodies. We see the marriage in his command of nature as he overwhelmed hunger, storms, and death. We see the marriage in the resurrection on Easter morning,[277] and as such, the Copernican picture actually fails as a complete and laudable metaphor. The picture the Christians offered was more like this:

o†

o†

Jesus is the kind of God who, seeing the dark places we are in, joins us[278] there. He does not allow us to continue spinning out in the darkness alone. He makes his dwelling with us, in our isolation, in our brokenness, in the cold spaces we make our homes.[279] But so, too, Jesus pursues our enemies. He moves toward them, seeking their good, and hoping for their restoration. Though we often see ourselves spinning out in the void, the dying and rising God is with us, and with everyone else.[280] The early Christian understanding encourages us to shift away from the old Copernican style picture. In the work of Jesus, they saw their God connecting all of reality to himself again. They saw their God instigating a new marriage. As such, they saw reality far more like this:

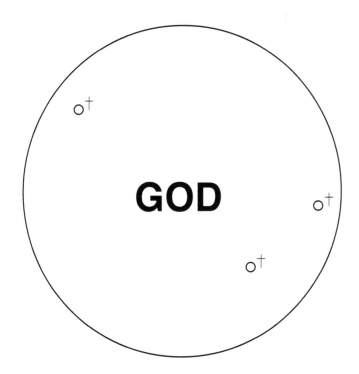

It's as though the enormity of the sun—which had been so distant for so long—had moved into our sphere and fully engulfed the earth. The good news is nothing less than the grand truth that God is here and heaven has come with him.[281] The resurrection is the event that unites and connects everything about our lives to the God who made us. Through the cross and resurrection, a massive door that had been closed was suddenly flung open and locked in place. Now, instead of us working to re-enter God's distant presence, we can know that he has defiantly entered ours.

I showed this picture to some friends of mine, and one who is still wrestling with the idea of Jesus looked at this picture for a long time. When she was ready she said to me, "I don't have to move, because he's here with me already."

That is faith.

That is the power through which someone's life is remade. Instead of seeing herself as alone, she saw her life and everything around her saturated with the presence of God. She began to live as though a great reconstruction was taking place. All her behaviors, all her ambitions, all her dreams and longings suddenly took on an everlasting quality. For years she had told been told by her religious friends that because of her past divorce, because of her doubts and questions she sat on the outside far from God. But none of it was true. Heaven was here and it had come for her.

THE SIGHT OF HEAVEN

One of my favorite photos is from the 1998 NBA Finals.[282] Chicago is playing game five in Utah. One more win will eliminate the Jazz and give the Bulls the title. The final seconds are clicking down, and Michael Jordan has the ball. He begins to drive, thrusts forward to the top of the key, then jerks back. His move puts the defender—one of the best in the game—on the floor. Jordan then pulls up, arches, and releases his final shot in a Bull's uniform.

The shutter snaps.

The photograph was taken from behind and in the distance we see the shot clock and rim. The ball hangs in the air, not yet reaching the basket. Four of the defenders on the floor stare up with a sickened look. Some of Jordan's teammates move toward the basket, but not Jordan. His body is relaxed as he descends to the floor.

The beauty of this picture is the crowd. Five or six hundred fans line the stands behind the backboard. A man is covering his nose and mouth with his hands. A few lean against their companions for comfort. Most just have wide eyes and half opened mouths, as though they've just seen a grievous car wreck. All the pictured faces are a mixture of distress and defeat.

Except one.

A child, ten years old or so, is on the left hand side about 6 rows up. His dad has boosted him in his arms so he can see. The boy's arms are outstretched. (They are the only arms raised in the photo except Jordan's.) His mouth is open—smiling and yelling something unknown. Joy pours forth from his face, and you can see prominently—in a field of purple and white Utah Jazz jerseys—his chest covered with a red and black "23."

Nothing is official yet, but everyone in that arena lives out their reality. Some see every reason for despondency. One with raised arms lives in bliss. Everyone reacts according to the glasses they wear—some purple, some red—and the glasses move them into the future.

If we are willing, we can choose to see heaven. We can choose to see it in the lives of those around us who are transformed, not by lucky flukes or genetics, but by the Spirit of God. We can choose to see it in the life and resurrection of Jesus, and we can see it in ourselves. We can choose to see places in our own story not as accidents, but as real encounters with God. This is heaven. It is here and it has come for us.

We make a mistake when we think of heaven as ever distant, un-experienced, and always a step beyond our lives now. The Bible is filled with stories, not of people being hurried out of here but of God descending and drawing the world to himself. In fact, the final chapters of the Bible end with a wedding of heaven and earth. God makes his home with us here, and what results is an entirely resurrected and repaired creation. As God himself says to close the Bible,

> "Look! God's dwelling place is now among the people, and he will dwell with them. They will be his people, and God himself will be with them and be their God. 'He will wipe every tear from their eyes. There will be no more death or mourning or crying or pain, for the old order of things [the present age] has passed away." He who was seated on the throne said, "I am making everything new!"[282]

Our hope for this day then is that we ourselves will be transformed into what we will always be, that "the one who began a good work in us will bring it to completion."[284] You and I have not yet arrived. We are not yet perfect. We are always in transit. Our lives are a work of tension, the tension between a work "begun" and a work "complete."[285]

As such, when we choose mercy over indifference, when we choose action over apathy, when we choose self-restraint and chastity over a life given over to our many reckless desires—we choose to live now as we will in the age to come. When we feed the hungry, clothe the naked, heal the sick, house the homeless, and die to ourselves for the sake of another, we enjoy the kingdom of heaven. When we hear the voice of God telling us that we are loved, that our many sins are forgiven, that we are his children, we experience now what we will experience forever. When we eat together, laugh together, sing together, serve together, take communion, love our enemies, and cancel debts, we choose to live the best kind of life—the life of God's future connected to him and to one another, in which evil and death are distant memories, and the world is flooded by the light and sustaining power of God.

Of course, Jesus is central to all this. He is not simply the one announcing a new kingdom. He is the King—the Christ, and in the landscape of prospective gods and goddess vying for our affection—he alone has a history of crushing misery and affliction in world altering ways. We see it in his miraculous signs that detail what is ahead. We see it in his deconstruction of those signs when he describes the world as a garden overrun with thorns and weeds which experiences a sudden harvest—in which both wheat and weeds are cut down, and the farmer brings all the wheat into his home, but the weeds are taken away and destroyed.[286] Jesus' stories and miracles point toward the end of evil in a unique and tangible way. In Jesus alone do we get the sense that repair may actually become a reality. We see the defeat of evil in the events of Good Friday and Easter, for the cross and resurrection are the sign to all that death could not and cannot overcome the life rising in God's Son.

THE AGE TO COME

On his first birthday, I bought my oldest son a copy of The Hobbit (which was only slightly less practical for a one year old than, say, a new car). The book sat on his shelf unblemished and unread until I brought it down a few weeks ago to look up a passage inside. On the first page I noticed something was written. It was an inscription—one in my own hand written a few years earlier. It said,

> To my beautiful son –
> I give you this book on your first birthday knowing that it will be years before we get to read it together. I greatly look forward to the days between now and then—getting to watch you grow, getting to hear you speak, getting to see what your heart is like.
>
> And some day, when you are able to understand, we will open the cover, and we will read this tale together for the first time. And you and I will journey into new worlds. Just as we journey together now.
> – Your companion and father

Since the births of my two boys, my highest desire in life has been to see them grow, to celebrate their victories, to lift their heads in trouble, to encourage in them strong minds and beautiful souls. I long for the day when we share common pleasures, when we take delight in a movie or a pitcher of beer, enjoy the same ski run or a great baseball game together. When I look at my two boys, I dream of them becoming the kind of men who can enjoy such treasures with me.

So too, this God has watched our births, watched us take our first few infantile steps. He has watched our many mistakes and helped to pick us up—though we may have been unaware. This God has watched to see our hearts and our growth, but just as a good father is not content for his little ones to remain little, we may assume God dreams of new days ahead. In the scope of God's future, our tale is just beginning. Perhaps God is pulling back the cover for the first time and leading us to that point where together we can look at the opening chapter and understand his kind of joys, his kind of delights, his dreams which color our world now and its future.

God has given us our lives and he alone has the power to sustain them, to grow them, to free them—to even resurrect them and pull us through death into his future. The only question is whether we will desire what he desires or cast that story aside.

The invitation has been sent. The door has been opened. It is simply up to us whether we will rise with him.

NOTES

263   See John 2:1-11 for the story.

264   John 2:1

265   (John 2:9) Which sure sounds like a divine title to me.

266   Numbers 13:26-27 among others.

267   Genesis 11:1-9. I would argue the act is so heartbreaking to God he confuses their languages *in order* to scatter the people so they might fulfill his first command to fill his good world and enjoy it (Genesis 1:28-30)

268   When for example, he calls the Jewish people to be "a kingdom of priests" in Exodus; this is an image of one people called to unite all the rest of humanity to God again. The image is again one of marriage.

269   Notice too, John often writes in the Chiastic form, a rhetorical technique popular in Greek literature and the Hebrew texts of the Bible in which, topically, the beginning of a section begins in the same place it end (see for example John 1:1-3 and John 1:14). These are the bookends of a structure that follows a pattern like A1, B1, C, B2, A2. John not only uses this practice in sections, he also adopts this technique for the overall structure of his biography. The first and last chapter detail those sent to testify, and the two chapters a step in (2 and 20) detail the resurrection. Chapters 3 and 19 deconstruct the meaning of the cross, and the movement continues inward.

270   John 20:11-18, contrasted by Mark 16:1, Luke 24:1, Matthew 28:1

271   So too, in John's story Jesus performed seven miracles—seven creative, world restoring acts. Seven, of course, is an important number. It is the number of days it took God to make the world.

272   John 20:1 The phrase is repeated in John 20:19.

273   Notice further how the timeline of Passion Week parallels Genesis. On Good Friday, God recreated humanity. Saturday he rested. On Sunday he entered his world to enjoy it.

274   Jesus says to Mary in the garden, "Go...to my brothers and tell them I am returning to my Father and your father, to my God and to your God." That may sound basic, but it is packed with meaning. "Up to this point Jesus has spoken about God as "*the* Father," or "the father who sent me," or "*my* father." He has called his followers "disciples" or "servants" or "friends." But now all that has changed! Look closely at verse 17: "Go to my brothers and say to them, 'I'm going up to my father and *your father*—to my God and *your God*.' (NT Wright). This community of people has been united to God in a new depth of relationship.

275   19 February 1473–24 May 1543

276   They saw Jesus in the writings of one of their ancient poets who, predicting a coming king, said, "The people walking in darkness have seen a great light; on those living in the land of deep darkness a light has dawned ... Every warrior's boot used in battle and every garment rolled in blood will be destined for burning, will be fuel for the fire. For to us a child is born, to us a son is given ... and he will be called Wonderful Counselor, Mighty God." (Isaiah 9:2-7)

277   So too we enjoy heaven uniting to our world "when we eat together, laugh together, sing together, and serve together ... when we clothe the naked, heal the sick, house the homeless, and die to ourselves for the sake of another ... when we listen to the scriptures, participate in Communion, love our enemies, and cancel debts ... More than anything, when we hear the voice of God telling us that we are loved, that our many sins are forgiven, that we are his children, we experience now what we will experience forever." (Jeff Cook. *Seven: The Deadly Sins and the Beatitudes.* Grand Rapids: Zondervan, 2008. P. 170).

278   As John said of Jesus, "The true light that gives light to everyone was coming into the world. He was in the world ... [He] became flesh and made his dwelling among us."

279 John 1:4-5, 14 among others.

280 This seems to me the central thesis advanced in Romans 1-3.

281 See Matthew 5:3-12 among many others.

282 Photo by Fernando Medina, Getty Images. http://a.espncdn.com/combiner/i?img=/photo/2010/0612/chi_g_jordan1x_576.jpg

283 Revelation 21:3-5

284 Philippians 1:6

285 See James Dunn. *Jesus and the Spirit: A Study of the Religious and Charismatic Experience of Jesus and the First Christians as Reflected in the New Testament.* Grand Rapids: Eerdmanns, 1997.

286 Matthew 13:24-29, 36-43

ACKNOWLEDGEMENTS

My deepest gratitude goes out to:

Angela Scheff who championed this book over and again.

Peter Kreeft, whose work has kept me sane. Many are marketed as the C.S. Lewis of our age, but my vote still has you firmly in that spot.

Tom Wright, who's writings have been pivotal for me.

TJ Wilson, Sarah Redman, Preston Sprinkle, Christine Meyers, Natalie and Justin Boyd who each read early drafts and whose thoughts and encouragements were very helpful!

Aaron Adamson who checked my writings on high level physics and basic cosmology. Any mistakes in the text on those fronts are his :)

Tammi VanDrunen, Tim Coons, Marte Samuelstein, and Kody Ziller who each have been exceptional sounding boards for the ideas here.

Scot McKnight for your many encouragements and constant advocacy.

Wes Morriston and Richard Blanke for being teachers of the highest order.

Mel Jensen for her outstanding editorial eye.

The fine people of Atlas (who are understandably tired of hearing about New Creation).

Betony Coons, Tony Garza, Shane White, and Emily Brink for the exceptional artistic work you have done on my behalf. You all are such treasures!

My students at UNC, who were often the first to wrestle through these issues with me.

And to Kelly. Who believes and suffers and continues to believe still.

SUB
VERSIVE
GREELEY, CO